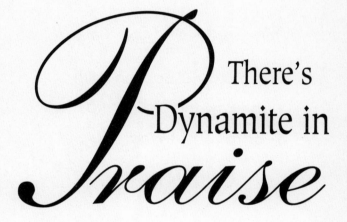

There's
Dynamite in
Praise

Other Books by Don Gossett

The Power of Spoken Faith

The Power of Your Words

What You Say Is What You Get

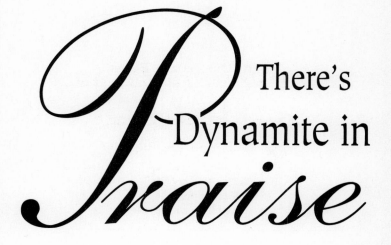

There's Dynamite in Praise

Don Gossett

WHITAKER
HOUSE

All Scripture quotations are taken from the King James Version (KJV) of the Holy Bible.

THERE'S DYNAMITE IN PRAISE

ISBN: 0-88368-644-9
Printed in the United States of America
© 1974 by Don Gossett

Whitaker House
30 Hunt Valley Circle
New Kensington, PA 15068
www.whitakerhouse.com

Library of Congress Cataloging-in-Publication Data

Gossett, Don, 1929–
There's dynamite in praise / by Don Gossett.
p.   cm.
ISBN 0-88368-644-9 (pbk.)
1. Praise of God. I. Title.
BV4817 .G67 2001
248.3—dc21
00-012128

3 4 5 6 7 8 9 10 11 12 ᴜᴊ 11 10 09 08 07 06 05 04

Contents

Introduction

∞

*I*n my travels as a missionary-evangelist, I've ministered to people who speak many different languages. But no matter where I go, I find that there is one word that is universally understood: the word *hallelujah*.

And how appropriate that God should have ordained this as the universal word! What an uplifting word! What blessed optimism! And what undreamed power lies hidden in those syllables!

The word means simply, "Praise the Lord." And it's a word that will be prominent in our vocabulary in heaven. John said in Revelation 19:1, *"I heard a great voice of much people in heaven, saying, Alleluia."* Again in verse 4, John said, *"And the four and twenty elders and the four beasts fell down and worshipped God that sat on the throne, saying, Amen; Alleluia."* And once again, in verse 6, John declared, *"I heard as it were the voice of a great multitude, and as the voice of many waters, and as the voice of mighty thunderings, saying, Alleluia."*

Perhaps you'll be surprised as you read in these pages about the power of praise. But every Christian needs to understand this secret and practice it. I pray that you will be greatly blessed as you respond to the challenge of this book.

—DON GOSSETT

Chapter 1

How I Discovered Praise Power

∞

Chapter 1

How I Discovered
Praise Power

∞

*I*was not raised in a Christian home, and I knew nothing of praise power until I was grown. I was born again in a fine Baptist church, was called to preach as a Baptist, and began my preaching ministry in Baptist churches.

My wife was raised in an old-fashioned Pentecostal home. Her dad has been for many years a real Holy-Spirit, pioneer Pentecostal preacher. So our backgrounds were very different.

Here I was a Baptist, my wife a Pentecostal. But we have come along wonderfully for years together. The Baptists stand for baptism in water; the Pentecostals stand for baptism in fire. You get water and fire together, and you produce steam. So we have been steaming along all of these blessed years!

A few weeks after Joy and I were married, however, I had an ego-shattering experience. I was working for evangelist William Freeman as his magazine editor. Realizing the importance of a deep devotional life, I would get up every morning and pray for an hour. Joy usually prayed at another time, and since our apartment was small, she couldn't help overhearing me.

"Honey," she said one day, with a mischievous twinkle in her eye, "I would suggest that one of these mornings you make a tape recording of your hour-long prayer. Then, instead of going through all the rigors of praying like that every morning, you could just turn the recorder on and let it play."

"What do you mean by that?' I replied, somewhat surprised.

"Honey," she said kindly, "I don't mean to embarrass you, but honestly, you say the same things every morning in exactly the same way, and it's just an hour of repetition."

"It is?" I asked in amazement. "I never thought of it that way."

"Well, you just think about it," she replied, going back to her work.

Some weeks later, in our evening prayer time that we always had together, Joy said, "Honey, the Lord has been so good to us, why don't we just devote this evening to praising the Lord, instead of asking? Let's just give Him thanks for all His benefits to us."

"A whole devotional time devoted to praise?" I thought. "I don't think I'm up to that!"

Furthermore, the very idea of praising God without asking Him for anything bothered me, just from a theological viewpoint. I had done a considerable amount of reading on the subject of prayer, and one of the authors I most admired taught the very practical view that prayer is made up of one basic essential: asking. He taught that while praise, thanksgiving, and singing are good, they are not the same as prayer. Prayer involves the simple process of asking and receiving. Now here was my wife suggesting we spend a whole devotional time not asking for anything—which in my mind was equivalent to not praying!

"No, Joy," I insisted. "We're going to pray. Praise is all right, but we have to pray."

"But, Honey," she protested, "isn't praising God the same as praying?"

"Not at all," I replied. "Prayer is asking. The answer to prayer is receiving. Praise is something else altogether."

"I don't know," she said doubtfully. "It seems that we hardly ever praise God."

"Joy, you just don't understand," I countered. "Why don't you get that book on prayer out of my library and read the chapter about asking? I'm sure it'll help you." Then, after a thoughtful pause, I said, "Now, let's get down to business here and start asking God to provide for our needs."

I was quite stubborn about it, and she went along with me. However, my wife had experienced a wonderful deliverance from a nervous disorder just before I met her. For eleven long months of her young life, she had been tormented by a mental oppression that had been a great trial to her.

"You're not going to live to see twenty-one," the Devil would torment her.

"What a terrible thought!" she'd reply within herself, not realizing the source of her thoughts.

"Yes, you're going to die," the Devil said unfeelingly, "and very soon!"

She'd cry and cry when those tormenting thoughts came, but nothing she did drove them away. She bought her clothes with the thought in mind that she would die young in life, and that possibly the dress she was buying would be among her burial clothes. The incredible thing about the Devil's ability is that he made her believe for a time that God was telling her she was going to die.

The nightly bouts of depression became unbearable. She began to think that if she were going to die so soon, she ought to stay awake and squeeze as much out of life as was left. She frittered away the nights doing this and that. Finally, knowing that she had to go to work in the morning, she'd try to get some rest. But by that time, she was too keyed up to sleep. So she'd spend the rest of the night tossing and turning, often struggling with cold chills and tormenting imaginations.

For eleven months, it was like living in a clear plastic bag. She could see everyone around her, but she was in a different world. From time to time, people peered in at her, but never quite understood her fears. On Sundays, she'd go to the First Assembly of God where her father was the pastor, and would play the piano and vibraharp. But her heart wasn't in it. Through the week, she tried to busy herself with the endless duties of her managerial position in a department store. But no matter how busy she was, still the haunting thought lingered in the back of her mind: "You're going to die soon. It won't be long now."

In desperation, she began a careful study of God's Word to see if she couldn't find an answer to her fears. Much to her delight, she found that God makes abundant promises to His people of long life, as well as all our hearts' desires. And since her desire was to invest her life in the Lord's service, she began to feel somewhat encouraged.

"But what if these thoughts about death really are coming from the Holy Spirit?" she'd ask herself. "What if God is trying to warn me?" So it became a seesaw existence. As long as she looked at the Word of God, she felt at peace. But when she allowed her attention to return to her old fears, nothing would give her any peace except the tranquilizers she'd been using.

"If only I could be sure that these thoughts about death are not from God!" she thought. But then it came to her very clearly one day that God would never speak anything to her by the Spirit that contradicts His Word. And the Word said very clearly that long, abundant life was her portion! It is the Devil who comes to kill, steal, and destroy! (See John 10:10.)

Gradually, as the Word of God did its work, Joy began to be free—not all the time, but as often as she wholeheartedly gave herself to the Word of God. In those times, she found herself praising God more and more. And the more she praised Him, the greater the victory she experienced.

The last depression she experienced happened on an Easter Sunday evening. Her grandmother had come to visit the family for the day. Easter Sunday was always a very busy day for Joy's family, and in the midst of all the hurry and scurry, hardly anybody noticed that Joy was in another of her dark times.

When they all went to church that evening, Joy was feeling about as low as anyone could feel. She played the piano as usual. And when it came time for the choir to sing, she played the vibraharp as beautifully as ever. But inside she was at the breaking point.

"Oh, God," she cried within herself, as she mechanically guided the mallets over the keyboard, "I can't stand anymore! I've done everything I know to do. I've prayed. I've fasted. I can't stand another service like this—nor another day of work! It's just too much, Lord!"

As soon as she finished playing her instrument, she sat down beside her grandmother on a front pew.

"Grandma, will you go home with me?" she whispered. "I'm really sick." Realizing that Joy must be quite troubled, she agreed to go. So the two of them tiptoed out of the service and walked the block and a half to the parsonage.

As soon as they entered the house, Joy went to her bedroom and threw herself across her bed, crying her heart out until there were no more tears to cry. Grandmother, realizing that Joy wanted to be alone, sat in the living room and prayed silently.

As Joy lay there pouring her heart out to God, again the Holy Spirit began to tell her to start praising God. She knew it was a crucial moment when the Lord was asking her to yield herself once and for all to a life of praise. This was her only way out.

"Here I am, Lord!" she cried. "I yield myself to You!" And from the depths of her being there welled up a mighty torrent of praise to God.

From that night on, Joy was free. No more tranquilizers were needed. Any time a cloud of depression came, she found that praising the Lord completely dispelled these spirits of gloom and heaviness.

So no wonder my young bride was sold on praise! And no wonder she found it difficult to understand my strange ideas about the distinctions to be carefully observed between praying and praising!

As she shared her experiences with me from time to time, finally the truth about the power of praise began to break across my spirit. I found myself going back to the Bible again and again to see if what she was saying was true. The more I searched, the more I was overwhelmed with the abundance of biblical teaching about the importance of praise. Finally, I began to agree to spend some of our devotional time in giving praise to God. Amazingly, I discovered greater blessings, more joy, and more marvelous things happening as we praised the Lord together.

I soon learned that prayer and praise are the two wings of spiritual power. There is no conflict. *"In every thing by prayer and supplication with thanksgiving let your requests be made known unto God,"* declared Paul in Philippians 4:6. Also, *"Continue in prayer, and watch in the same with thanksgiving"* (Colossians 4:2). So as I opened my heart to the Word, slowly I began to drop my prejudices against praise, and I discovered some tremendous workings of God in my life.

I encountered this great Scripture: *"Thou art holy, O thou that inhabitest the praises of Israel"* (Psalm 22:3). The Lord inhabits our praises. That is, the Lord manifests Himself as we praise Him. The word *inhabits* means "to live in, dwell in." So this was a revelation to my heart—that the mighty God dwells in, lives in, manifests Himself in our praises.

I will always thank God that He used my lovely bride to guide me into this praising principle. Now, after these many years, the Lord has kept my wife's nervous system strong. She has given birth to our five healthy children, she has had two very critical miscarriages, and through it all her nerves have been strong and well. Any time Satan has sought to afflict her nervous system, we have courageously employed praise power, and God has responded by healing those nerves.

I have often said that no person will ever have a nervous breakdown who practices praise power. Why? Because God inhabits our praises, and where God is working, no nervous condition can prevail. Fear, worry, grief, frustration—all of these negative factors that help produce a nervous breakdown are forced out through joyful praise to God.

I've never known a Christian who practices praise power to land in a mental hospital. Praise is so harmonious with God's expectation of us that it is the power that makes our lives fragrant with heaven's best.

Chapter 2

Praising God Continually

∽

Chapter 2

Praising God Continually

∞

One of my first experiences of the power of praise came during the first year my wife and I were married. We were driving to the West Coast, when our car had motor trouble in the mountains. Not possessing mechanical ability, I was unable to get the car going again.

Then along came a man who was a mechanic, and I thought he would be able to get the car rolling again. After much effort, he gave up. He did offer to push my car with his in an attempt to get the motor active.

After a few miles of pushing me up that mountain, he honked his horn and motioned me off the highway. He explained that he could push me no farther, as his car was heating up. He then offered to send a tow truck to tow me to a garage. Upon inquiry, I found that it was 45 miles to the nearest town, and the towing service would be $2 per mile. That totaled $90, and I had only $15 left for the remainder of my trip.

I thanked the man for all his efforts, but told him my wife and I would have to do something else in our dilemma.

That "something else" was to turn to the Lord. We got out our Bibles and began to read. After about 15 minutes of Bible reading on that lonely mountainside, we felt the Word had inspired our faith adequately to ask God for a miracle.

With our whole hearts we asked God to undertake for that dead motor. Never can I forget the thrill that came to me when I turned on the ignition, stepped on the starter, and the motor started right up! How happy I was as I zoomed up that mountain at 50 miles an hour!

I was praising God with a loud voice, until suddenly the motor coughed and started dying again. When it started dying, so did my praises.

My wife said quietly, "Honey, it is easy to praise God when all is going well; why don't we sacrifice praise to God?"

I pulled the car to the side of the road and asked God to forgive me for my sin of inconsistency: praising God when the car was running well, but ceasing to praise Him when the car acted up again.

After we'd sacrificed praises to God for some time, we continued on our journey. During those last 450 miles to our destination, the motor cut out a few times more and gave indication it was stopping again. But I just praised God all the stronger each time, and we made it all right that night. There is power in praise.

This does not mean that everything that comes along is of God; it simply means that we give thanks to God for the assurance that whatever the problem, God has the solution! Hallelujah!

The more I experimented with the power of praise, the more I kept digging into the Scriptures to see what else I could find out about the subject.

One day I was sitting at my desk when I came across a verse in Hebrews 13 that arrested my attention: *"By him therefore let us offer the sacrifice of praise to God continually, that is, the fruit of our lips giving thanks to his name"* (verse 15).

"How could anybody praise God continually?" I asked myself in bewilderment. "I can see that it's good to praise God, but surely not all the time!"

Knowing that the best way to interpret any given verse of Scripture is to study its context, I began to think about the basic message of the book of Hebrews. I recalled the many contrasts that the author pointed out between the Old and New Testament priesthoods, blood offerings, and sacrifices. In all these matters, the promises of God through Jesus Christ are better than the old covenant.

The improvement was especially apparent in the area of sacrifices. Whereas the smoke of Old Testament sacrificial offerings ascended from the altar continually, now in New Testament times the one sacrifice of Jesus made all other sacrifices unnecessary.

"But wait a minute!" I said. "It's only a partial truth to say that God doesn't require sacrifices anymore. True, He doesn't require sacrifices for sin, but He does require sacrifices of praise. That's what it says here: *'Let us offer the sacrifice of praise to God.'"*

I hesitated a moment before I added that troublesome word: *"continually."* Thinking that maybe, just maybe, there might be a faulty translation here, I decided to see if I could find any other passages that might shed some light on the subject. I did! I found Psalm 34:1: *"I will bless the LORD at all times: his praise shall continually be in my mouth."*

"Not again!" I fumed. "That's even clearer than Hebrews 13:15! And if David was blessing and praising God at all times in Old Testament days, then what's wrong with me? Why don't I praise God more than I do?"

"Watch out!" another voice warned. "You don't want to make a fanatic out of yourself, do you?"

Immediately I recalled several Christian friends I'd known who had made spectacles of themselves by continually praising God. When you met them on the street, the first thing they'd say was "Praise the Lord!" They'd even say it in a restaurant or a bank, and it embarrassed me to be seen with them.

But then I began to say to myself, "But praising the Lord too much isn't my problem; my problem is not praising Him enough!"

"Mmmm, now, I don't know about that," that other voice replied. "You praise God a lot more than most people."

"But that's not the point!" I insisted. "God says here that we're to offer the sacrifice of praise continually, not just once in a while."

I tilted my chair back on two legs and just sat there and thought for a while. And, believe me, I had something to think about! God was telling me that

He wanted me to live a life of praise. He wanted me to praise Him while I was driving and while I was filling out my tax forms. He wanted me to praise Him while I was taking out the garbage and while I was taking a bath. He wanted me to praise Him in good times and bad. Anytime. All the time.

"All right, Lord," I said finally. "If that's what You want, who am I to say no?" And I made a covenant with God then and there that I would begin praising Him in all things.

That was a major breakthrough, although I can't say that I fully understood the mystery of praise and why it unleashed such great power in my life. Not until some time later did it become a little clearer.

One day I was drawn back to Hebrews 13:15. As I read it over again, I noticed that the writer defined praise as *"the fruit of our lips giving thanks to his name."* The word *"fruit"* caught my attention. I remembered how Jesus had said, *"Herein is my Father glorified, that ye bear much fruit"* (John 15:8). While there are many ways in which we may bear fruit as Christians, here is one sure way: by *"the fruit of our lips giving thanks to his name."* Every time we give thanks and praise to the Lord, we are bearing fruit. The more we praise Him, the more fruit we bear. The more fruit we bear, the more the Father is glorified! And the more the Father is glorified, the more His power is unleashed.

Another term that interested me in the passage in Hebrews was the word *"sacrifice."* We are to offer the sacrifice of praise to God. That suggested that we are not to praise God only when all is going well. We are to praise Him continually. Even when we do not feel like it, we are to sacrifice praise.

That is what God wants. When circumstances are dismal and gloomy, sacrifice praise. When sickness strikes our bodies and our will power is reduced to nil, sacrifice praise.

I knew I had found a key Bible truth. God commands us to offer to Him the sacrifice of praise continually, feelings or no feelings. Good days and bad days, in fair or foul weather, whether we are up or down, in sickness and in health: sacrifice praise.

It came to me with fresh impact that praise is not optional for the Christian. God expects it of us. He expected it of me. I was not doing God a big favor by praising Him; I was simply obeying Him.

Sometimes we encounter objections from men that praise is fanatical, emotional, or unmannerly. But we do not offer praise to please men. We know that *"whoso offereth praise glorifieth me* [God]" (Psalm 50:23). Our praises always glorify the Lord.

Of course, it is possible to offer praise insincerely, mechanically. But real heart praise unto God always glorifies Him.

And it is not sufficient to say, "Well, I praise the Lord in my heart." That is good. But God wants us to use our voices to praise Him. Vocal praise is what God requires. *"O bless our God, ye people, and make the voice of his praise to be heard"* (Psalm 66:8).

For Practical Application

Here is a simple ten-point outline with supporting Scriptures, which will be a practical help to you in learning to praise God at all times. I suggest you commit this material to memory, and quote it aloud when you are feeling depressed, discouraged, or indifferent. Then act on the instructions of the Scriptures, and victory will be yours!

1. God's command for New Testament Christians: *"By him therefore let us offer the sacrifice of praise to God continually, that is, the fruit of our lips giving thanks to his name"* (Hebrews 13:15).

2. The vow of David, the man after God's own heart: *"I will bless the LORD at all times: his praise shall continually be in my mouth"* (Psalm 34:1).

3. The practice of the first Christians: *"And* [they] *were continually in the temple, praising and blessing God"* (Luke 24:53).

4. The will of God for every Christian: *"In every thing give thanks: for this is the will of God in Christ Jesus concerning you"* (1 Thessalonians 5:18).

5. A vital proof of the true Spirit-filled life: *"Be filled with the Spirit....Giving thanks always for all things unto God and the Father in the name of our Lord Jesus Christ"* (Ephesians 5:18, 20).

6. The chief function of the royal priesthood: *"But ye are a chosen generation, a royal priesthood, an holy nation, a peculiar people; that ye should show forth the praises of him who hath called you out of darkness into his marvellous light"* (1 Peter 2:9).

7. The way Bible believers begin every gathering: *"Enter into his gates with thanksgiving, and into his courts with praise: be thankful unto him, and bless his name"* (Psalm 100:4).

8. A message to be heeded from the throne: *"And a voice came out of the throne, saying, Praise our God, all*

ye his servants, and ye that fear him, both small and great" (Revelation 19:5).

9. The Christian's obligation as long as he has breath: *"Let every thing that hath breath praise the* Lord. *Praise ye the* Lord*"* (Psalm 150:6).

10. A habit to be practiced all day long: *"From the rising of the sun unto the going down of the same the Lord's name is to be praised"* (Psalm 113:3).

Chapter 3

When All Else Fails, Try Praising

∞

Chapter 3

When All Else Fails,
Try Praising
∞

*I*was invited to speak at a church that had undergone deep testing. Satan had assaulted this church with confusion, division, and defeat. Before the morning service, several people spoke to me about the great anxiety of their hearts for their church.

"We've not had a soul saved in our church for over a year," one lady told me.

Another one said, "Our services have been dry and barren for so long."

"Our young people are indifferent to the Gospel and the workings of the Spirit," declared an elderly Christian.

Yet all of these people told me how they had been praying and crying out to God to send revival to their church. One said they had been meeting part of a day each week for intercession on behalf of their dilemma. This had gone on for about two years. Yet everything registered failure in their church activities.

That morning I preached on "Affirming God's Promises by Praise." I challenged this sincere group of people that God's promises are "yea and amen in Christ Jesus." (See 2 Corinthians 1:20.) I assured them it was not the will of their heavenly Father for them to go on defeated.

When I came to the close of my message, I shared with them this dynamic Scripture: *"Continue in prayer, and watch in the same with thanksgiving"* (Colossians 4:2). I told them that continual prayer for their needs was not wrong, but now was the time for them to take their answer by offering thanks for God's guarantees to bless, save souls, and send revival.

I invited everyone to join with me in fervent prayer, acting upon Matthew 18:19, *"that if two of you shall agree on earth as touching any thing that they shall ask, it shall be done for them of my Father which is in heaven."* We agreed in prayer that the Father would work by His Spirit to save souls that night! Then we agreed for a spiritual refreshing to the people.

I also encouraged everyone to embrace with me Mark 11:24: *"What things soever ye desire, when ye pray, believe that ye receive them, and ye shall have them."* We desired souls to be saved, for God to bless us with the manifestation of His presence. So I told the people to *believe* we received those things, and to thank God we had them. By believing, the things we desired were ours!

I encouraged everyone to lift hands with me in an act of faith and give thanks to God for granting the things for which we had just asked, and for which they had been asking for so long.

I then read Colossians 4:2 again, emphasizing the latter part, *"Watch in the same with thanksgiving."*

"Now people," I said, "throughout the afternoon I want you to do some watching for this service. I want you to watch with thanksgiving, just like the Bible commands. Every time you think of our service tonight, look up and thank God for saving souls, healing sick bodies, blessing, and meeting needs."

The people were stirred to go out and do that very thing: Watch with thanksgiving!

Many of them told me later that night how they had done just that. One lady said, "Normally during the afternoon, I would weep for our church, and beg God to undertake. But this afternoon, instead of being anxious about our meeting, I just held my heart steady and strong by praising the Lord. I kept watching with thanksgiving."

And God, who watches over His Word to perform it, certainly responded to us that night! Even before the main service was underway, two young people were convicted of their sins and their need of Christ, right at the youth service prior to the evangelistic meeting. Both accepted Christ!

Six more were converted in the evangelistic service when I preached. What rejoicing there was that night, after eight souls were born again! The Lord confirmed His Word *"with signs following"* (Mark 16:20), and everyone who entered into the service was abundantly blessed.

All agreed that it was our "watch with thanksgiving" that produced such heavenly manifestations. Yes, we can pray and pray and pray, but we must believe God's Word. By thanksgiving, *take* what He has provided. Hallelujah!

What about your needs? Have you asked, prayed, and begged God? Now is the time for you to begin offering thanks by faith for what God has promised.

I charge you to give yourself to "watching with thanksgiving." You have surely prayed long enough. Thank God for doing exactly what He has promised to do, and I assure you, God will respond.

"Thou art holy, O thou that inhabitest the praises of Israel" (Psalm 22:3).

In 1955, I was conducting evangelistic meetings at a church in Willamina, Oregon. On the closing Sunday, we had a record-breaking Sunday school attendance.

Pastor Harry Olsen asked me to prepare to speak to the whole group in the main auditorium of the church, for there were many unsaved people present.

At the appointed time, I spoke to the people, including the many unsaved visitors, about Jesus Christ, salvation, heaven, hell, and related subjects. I made a firm invitation for the unsaved to accept Christ that morning. We sang "Just As I Am" and waited for sinners to come to Christ. Sadly, no one responded.

I appealed again, being deliberate and forceful in presenting the claims of the Gospel to them. We sang "Softly and Tenderly Jesus Is Calling." Again to my keen disappointment, not a person moved toward the front to receive Christ as personal Savior.

I knew there were many who needed Christ, and I refused to stop that invitation in failure. So with all the urgency I could muster, I told them of the love of God, the grace of Jesus, and the calling of the Holy Spirit to them—that day. We sang another invitation, and I stood there stunned by the lack of response.

I bowed silently for prayer on the platform, asking the Holy Spirit for guidance. Suddenly this Scripture flashed into my mind: *"Thou art holy, O thou that inhabitest the praises of Israel"* (Psalm 22:3).

With this guidance of the Holy Spirit, I then asked every Christian in the auditorium to join me in an offering of vocal praise to the Lord. At first many Christians were reluctant to praise the Lord, especially with so many visitors in the church. But I continued to lead the people in this wonderful offering of praise that mightily pleases the Lord.

Actually, the true spirit of praise doesn't drive people away: it attracts them. In Acts 2:47 the early Christians were *"praising God, and having favour with all the people. And the Lord added to the church daily such as should be saved."* People desire reality in Christ. They don't want a dead tradition, a worthless formality. People crave reality. When we praise the Lord, we are not being obnoxious or disorderly. Praises to the

Lord are beautiful, harmonious with heaven, pleasing to God.

As we praised the Lord that morning, the Spirit of God hovered on that service in mighty power. Suddenly, without any further pleading on my part, unsaved people began to come to Christ. Men, women, and young people came to Jesus for salvation. Tears were streaming down the faces of sinners as they made their way forward.

I stood back, amazed at what I was witnessing. God was inhabiting our praises, and souls were being saved—many of them.

At the close of that glorious invitation, we counted more than 20 people who had joyfully accepted Christ that morning!

It is always right to praise the Lord. *"Whoso offereth praise glorifieth me"* (Psalm 50:23). Every time we praise Him, we glorify His name.

Someone may ask, "What about the Scripture that says *'let all things be done decently and in order'*?" What about it? That's 1 Corinthians 14:40. All things in worship are to be done *"decently and in order."*

But tell me, please, is there anything disorderly about praising God? Praise is God's order. Man's order in religious worship may be ceremonial, ritualistic, formal. But God's order is dignity, life, and liberty. There is absolutely nothing undignified about praising the Lord. Nor is there anything indecent about praising the Lord!

When all else fails, praise prevails. Human persuasion, begging with tears, and all else often fails to produce anticipated results. But praise never fails to bring God's response to us, with our needs and circumstances.

Why does praise prevail? Because God inhabits our praises! Remember, praise is the language of faith, and faith is the victory (1 John 5:4).

If you are sick, begin to praise the Lord, saying, "By His stripes I am healed." (See Isaiah 53:5.) You can't say "Praise the Lord" ten times without a smile coming to your face, and your circumstances being changed. Multitudes have been healed by praising the Lord.

Dr. John Lucas, Sr., has been a veteran minister for many years across Canada. He is now past 90 years of age at this time, and going strong for his Lord. I asked Brother Lucas his secret of such strength and vibrancy at his age. Pastor Lucas told me, "The reason God has kept me in good health is that I praise the Lord often. Yes, praising the Lord is the reason I've enjoyed such benefits from the Lord."

It is sometimes a characteristic of elderly people to become grumpy and whiny in their advanced years. But I've met many elderly Christians who have learned, like Pastor Lucas of Calgary, Alberta, to praise the Lord; and God keeps them cheerful and bright for Him.

Often when I preach on the blessings of praise, I emphasize the tremendous benefits that come to those who praise the Lord daily. And while the benefits of praise are abundant, we miss the mark if we praise Him for benefits only.

I praise the Lord because I believe in praise. God's Word abounds with hundreds of challenging Scriptures that call me to praise the Lord.

I believe it is a good thing to praise the Lord often. I believe God is immensely pleased with our praises.

I believe I am in the center of God's perfect will when I am giving Him thanks in everything. I believe this is the sacrifice God wants of me: to praise Him continually.

Yes, I actually believe in my heart of hearts that praising the Lord is right, scriptural, God-pleasing, and an evidence of the true Spirit-filled life.

I believe that in heaven we will join the redeemed of all ages in praising the Lamb who was slain for us. Praise is the heavenly language. I believe I draw my heart heavenward every time I employ my heart and lips in praising the Lord.

If you believe in praise, then join me. *"O magnify the LORD with me, and let us exalt his name together"* (Psalm 34:3).

As long as I live it will be a rule engraved on my tongue to bring praise like fruit for an offering and my lips as a sacrificial gift. I will make skillful music with lyre and harp to serve God's glory, and the flute of my lips will I raise in praise of His rule of righteousness. Both morning and evening I will enter into the covenant of God: and at the end of both I will recite His commandments, and so long as they continue to exist, there will be my frontier and my journey's end. Therefore I will bless His name in all I do, before I move hand or foot, whenever I go out or come in, when I sit down and when I rise, even when lying on my couch, I will chant His praise.

My lips will praise Him as I sit at the table that is set for all, and before I lift my hand to partake of any nourishment from the delicious fruits of the earth.

When fear and terror come, and there is only anguish and distress, I will still bless and thank Him for His wondrous deeds, meditate upon His power, and lean upon His mercies all day long. For I know that in His hand is justice for all that live, and all His works are true. So when trouble comes, or salvation, I praise Him just the same.

—*Praising God at All Times*
(Column X, *Manual of Discipline,*
Dead Sea Scrolls)

Chapter 4

So You'd Rather Praise in Private?

∞

Chapter 4

So You'd Rather Praise in Private?

∞

*O*ne of the biggest problems many of us face in praising the Lord openly is that of overcoming our natural inhibitions. We almost feel embarrassed to praise God, simply because nobody else is doing it. And all of us understand how difficult it is to do a thing that no one else is doing, especially if it is quite certain that the doing of that thing will bring ridicule from others.

I recall a childhood incident that illustrates this point. During the Depression, our family was often embarrassed by many things—but then almost everybody was poor, so the embarrassment was bearable. But I remember that my dad finally got an electrician's job in Enid, Oklahoma, so we moved there, thinking our circumstances might soon improve.

However, it wasn't long until he lost the job, and we were compelled to move back to our old home. The trip had to be made by bus, and Dad had only enough money to buy tickets for my mother, my sister, and me. (My little brother was able to go free.)

"But how will you get home?" mother asked anxiously.

"I'll hitchhike," Dad replied. "It won't take long."

So he took us to the Enid bus station, where we were to wait until our bus arrived. My dad, however, left on foot for the edge of Enid, carrying his heavy electrician's gear.

About an hour later, we boarded the bus for our journey home. When we arrived at the outskirts of Enid, on the main highway leading out of the city, I suddenly spotted my dad standing beside the highway, hitchhiking.

When I saw him, I sprang from my seat and exclaimed, "That's my daddy!" My mother was most embarrassed by my excitement, because she felt badly that my dad had to hitchhike home while we rode the bus.

But I was proud to see my dad, and I said it again, "There's my daddy," as the bus rolled past where he was standing.

Everyone on that bus knew that was my father. And probably everyone knew why he was hitchhiking—but I didn't care. I was too young to realize how embarrassing this was to my mother. I only knew that I loved my daddy and was mighty proud that he had paid the price for my ride home.

When I was twelve years old, I came to the solemn realization of what Jesus paid for me when He gave His life for my sins, took my place on the cross, and gave me a place in heaven forever. But not until many years later, through the gentle ministry of my wife, did the Holy Spirit strip away the inhibitions that kept me from praising Jesus without embarrassment. I'm glad that I can now say that I'm proud of Jesus. I love to brag on Him and tell others about His glories.

D. L. Moody once told of an elderly man who gave a public testimony at one of his meetings. He had lived most of his life on "Grumble Street," he said. But after he became a Christian he moved to "Thanksgiving Street." Even in his advanced years of accepting Christ, he was full of thanks to the Lord who had saved his soul. The joy of gratitude was written all over his face.

Often we should take inventory here and ask ourselves this personal question: Do I have a thankful heart? If we do not, we are hardly worthy of the name *Christian.*

But true thanksgiving is not complete until it is expressed. It must become vocal. Some excuse themselves by saying, "I am grateful in my heart." That's good, but it is not acceptable to Jesus. Praise must be expressed openly. Remember the ten lepers of Luke 17? (See verses 11–19.)

There is so much discouragement in this world. Most of us are quick to complain but slow to give thanks to God.

I believe that many people who need healing today would be completely delivered if gratitude toward God were expressed. And especially those afflictions of the spirit nature (fear, worry, burdens, depression) would be healed every time we would offer praise to the Lord.

I ask you, friend, where do you live? If you live on Thanksgiving Street, you are a healthy person, spiritually sound. Satan seeks to get us to focus our attention on our problems, pains, and persecutions. In doing so, we cease being praisers of the Lord, but become fretters about our problems.

One of the sobering facts of life is that we have enemies: people who criticize us, find fault with us, and seek to demoralize us. But *"if God be for us, who can be against us?"* (Romans 8:31). We know we are Christians by the grace of God. When we consider His love, we should turn to the Lord in an overflow of thanksgiving.

Friend, if just now you are chafing under the cruel blows of criticism, breathe a prayer for your critic, then turn to the Lord in praise, and I assure you that the spirit of praise will revive your disturbed heart and give you the inner assurance of victory in your Lord!

Chapter 5

First Praise—Then Increase

Chapter 5

First Praise—Then Increase

∽

*P*raising God is the secret of having increased blessings in your life. Therefore I would suggest that you take the following verses as key principles to live by every day of your life: *"Let the people praise thee, O God; let all the people praise thee. Then shall the earth yield her increase; and God, even our own God, shall bless us"* (Psalm 67:5–6).

When we praise the Lord, *then* increase, abundance, and provisions come, and God will bless us. If you need God to undertake for you in your deficient living, begin to praise the Lord; *then* you will experience increase. God promises it. And God *"cannot lie"* (Titus 1:2).

God will bless us *after* we praise the Lord. Not only when all is well. Not just when we are perfectly healthy and sound. Not only when all our bills are paid. But right in our adversities—that's the time we praise the Lord. Then God will bless us.

There is a story that tells of two angels who come from heaven every morning and go on their rounds all day long. One is the Angel of Requests. The other is the Angel of Thanksgiving. Each carries a basket. The basket belonging to the Angel of Requests is soon filled to overflowing, for everyone pours into it great handfuls of requests; but when the day is ended the Angel of Thanksgiving has in his basket only two or three small contributions of gratitude.

One fact that the Spirit of God has burned into my heart again and again is this one: Most people miss the tremendous power of praise.

A missionary in China was living a defeated life. Everything about him seemed to be touched with sadness. Although he prayed many months for victory over depression and discouragement, no answer came. His life remained quite the same. He determined to leave his post and go to an interior station where he could be quiet and spend long hours in prayer until victory was assured. Upon reaching the place, he was entertained in the home of a fellow missionary. On the wall of his bedroom hung this motto: "Try thanksgiving."

The two words gripped his heart, and he thought within himself, "Have I been praying all these months and not been praising?" He stopped and began to praise the Lord, and was greatly uplifted. Instead of hiding away to agonize in prayer, he returned immediately to his waiting native converts to tell them about praise power. Wonderful blessing resulted from his testimony, and the native converts were encouraged to begin praising the Lord. Many bondages were broken as a result.

Mrs. Charles Cowman tells of the power of praise in her own experience:

> It was a dark, dark night in my life when the words *"Praise waiteth for thee, O God, in Sion"* (Psalm 65:1) were impressed upon my mind. I had been waiting in prayer for months. The months were now stretching into years— piled up, as it were, before God. Couldn't I now wait in praise before I saw the answer, or must I wait for signs and wonders before I believed His Word? God was waiting for me to take this final step in faith, and when I began to praise Him for the answer, to wait in praise, to *"rest in the LORD, and wait patiently for him"* (Psalm 37:7), He began to answer in a manner that was *"exceeding abundantly above all"* that I could ask or think (Ephesians 3:20). The possession of the secret of victory has transformed my life and filled it with unutterable gladness.

Remember: Prayer asks. Praise takes, or obtains, the answer.

But when we come to pray, there is often the experience of the Enemy making us "sin-conscious," with a keen sense of unworthiness. This is a real damper to effective prayer. So before we do anything else in approaching God, we are commanded to *"enter into his gates with thanksgiving, and into his courts with praise: be thankful unto him, and bless his name. For the LORD is good"* (Psalm 100:4–5). Start positively in approaching our wonderful and holy God, by praising Him.

Have you ever met a Christian whom you really like to be around? That person has probably learned the secret of praising the Lord. I know there are so many who go around with sour attitudes toward life, and expressions on their faces that look as though they had been weaned on dill pickles. But those who have vitality and zest for living have learned the secret of praising God. When we learn this lesson of praising the Lord often, we have learned the secret of one of the most satisfying experiences of life.

A woman approached me at the close of a Sunday night rally at the Queen Elizabeth Playhouse in Vancouver, where I had just preached. She looked cynical, worried, frowning. She told me how she had sought healing, but to no avail. What should she do?

"First of all, you need to start being a joyful Christian, for the joy of the Lord is your strength," I said to her. "I've noticed you all evening with a sad countenance. If Jesus has saved you, He will change your life. He will put a spring in your step, a song in your heart, a smile on your face, and will give you a zest for living."

I continued, "When you get home with these two ladies who came with you, I want the three of you to sit down and begin saying slowly, sincerely, 'Praise the Lord,' ten times. If you don't have a smile on your face by the end of that, you will probably never smile at anything. It is impossible to say 'Praise the Lord' and frown. Try it. It just won't come out."

Whether they took my advice or not, I do not know, as I never saw them again. But this much I know: this advice has worked for me. I have never been quite so joyful a Christian as I've been since I learned to praise the Lord.

Practice praise power! Praising God has power to lift your spirit, loose you from your bondages, and give you victory in every circumstance. *"Rejoice in the Lord alway: and again I say, Rejoice"* (Philippians 4:4).

Do we as Christians realize that there is due to God from our lips *"the sacrifice of praise to God continually"* (Hebrews 13:15)? Have we endeavored to measure up to the expectation of God, *"In every thing give thanks, for this is the will of God in Christ Jesus concerning you"* (1 Thessalonians 5:18)?

So many ask and keep asking of God, but are slow in the matter of acknowledging the blessings God has so bountifully given and promised. Surely this would not continue if we realized how precious to God are His people's praises.

O come, let us sing unto the LORD*: let us make a joyful noise to the rock of our salvation. Let us come before his presence with thanksgiving, and make a joyful noise unto him with psalms.* (Psalm 95:1–2)

Be glad in the LORD*, and rejoice, ye righteous: and shout for joy, all ye that are upright in heart.* (Psalm 32:11)

Rejoice evermore. (1 Thessalonians 5:16)

Let every thing that hath breath praise the LORD*.* (Psalm 150:6)

It is a good thing to give thanks unto the LORD*, and to sing praises unto thy name, O most High.* (Psalm 92: 1)

> *Ye are a chosen generation, a royal priesthood, an holy nation, a peculiar people; that ye should show forth the praises of him who hath called you out of darkness into his marvellous light* (1 Peter 2:9)

If I had never received a single benefit from praise, I still would know it is right. God's Word abounds with this subject from cover to cover.

Praise power has brought so many wonderful benefits. When the Lord made Himself real to me as a teenager, He planted in my heart to sing often, "Thank you, Lord, for saving my soul." Oh, the wonder of His love as I would sing to Him over and over this beautiful chorus!

In San Francisco, praise power brought to me a magnificent baptism of the Spirit, with the initial physical evidence of speaking in other tongues. Appropriately, this mighty baptism came to me on Thanksgiving Day!

Praise power brought a miraculous healing to my wife when she was dying with rheumatic fever in 1953.

Praise power broke the bands of poverty in those days and brought God's supply of our material needs.

Praise power has brought so many personal benefits. When X-rays revealed I had a critically enlarged heart in 1949, praise power brought an instantaneous deliverance.

If I were you who are sick, I would daily stand my ground boldly and fearlessly, rebuking the Enemy in the name of Jesus. Then practice praise power. Praise the Lord by repeating this Scripture: "By His stripes I am healed." (See Isaiah 53:5.) That is honoring Jesus for what He has provided. Praise Jesus for what He has given. Remember: first praise—then increase.

If I were you who have unsaved loved ones in your family, I would embrace this promise of Acts 16:31: *"Believe on the Lord Jesus Christ, and thou shalt be saved, and thy house."* Begin to praise the Lord for the saving of your loved ones. I've known over 3000 conversions to Christ as people have embraced this promise and acted out their faith by praising God, until the answer came and the loved ones came to Christ!

If I were you who are oppressed by fear, I would praise the Lord aloud and declare the liberating truth of 2 Timothy 1:7: *"God hath not given us the spirit of fear; but of power, and of love, and of a sound mind."*

If I were struggling with a bad habit, such as smoking or drinking, I would praise the Lord for deliverance even before the habit was broken. Your practice of praise power manifests the forces that will break every chain and bring abundance of blessing.

Chapter 6

Praise: The Key to Power

Chapter 6

Praise: The Key to Power

∞

*I*n my travels on the North American conti-
nent and across the seas, I've ministered to
many races of people who speak different languages. However, one happy thing I've always discovered among God's people is that the English word
that is the very essence of praise is found almost
unchanged in every language. That's the word *hallelujah,* which is indeed the universal word.

The word *hallelujah* means literally, "Praise the
Lord." It is one of the most common words in the
Bible, for it appears hundreds of times in God's Word.
For example, the last five psalms begin and end
with the words, *"Praise ye the LORD,"* which means
"hallelujah." It would be a good thing if our speech
always began and ended the same way each day—
with praising the Lord!

It is proper to use our tongues for praise, to
obey the oft-repeated command of Psalm 107:31: *"Oh
that men would praise the LORD for his goodness, and*

for his wonderful works to the children of men." We can, of course, use our tongues in other ways if we choose. Some men use them to curse and blaspheme. Christians shrink from using their tongues in such a way, but some do use their tongues in other ways that are not pleasing to the Lord.

For instance, to use your tongue in grumbling, complaining, criticizing, gossiping—these uses of the tongue grieve the Lord.

If you choose to use your tongue in negative, gloomy talk, all you will get is a pickle-like disposition and a sour-faced appearance, which will make you unwelcome company to others.

I want to challenge you to this "hallelujah living," this praising principle, that will keep your life full of joy and blessings. Take note of the following characteristics of praise.

1. Praise works wonders. Many of God's people today have discovered the secret that God's people learned long ago. When King Jehoshaphat appointed singers to say, *"Praise the Lord; for his mercy endureth for ever"* (2 Chronicles 20:21), then the Lord fought on behalf of His people. Yes, praise still produces blessed victory—today!

2. Praise is the secret of faith. The Bible is clear that faith is all-important in receiving healing, and true faith contains the vital element of praise. When you believe with all your heart that "by his stripes I am healed" (see Isaiah 53:5), you will praise the Lord by faith as much as if you had already received. And God honors that kind of faith. Hundreds have submitted testimonials to us that they have been completely healed by declaring

with their whole hearts, "Thank You, Jesus; by Your stripes I am healed!"

3. Praise precedes the baptism of the Spirit. God does not baptize grouches. I've heard many hundreds of baptized believers testify that the victory came as they praised God for the gift of the Holy Spirit by faith. I've often witnessed the same in our meetings. Before Pentecost, the 120 were *"continually...praising and blessing God"* (Luke 24:53). It is the same today: praise to God gets us near to Him who is the Baptizer. A continual flow of praise characterizes the one who is truly Spirit-filled (Ephesians 5:18–20).

4. Praise brings God's response. Psalm 22:3 assures us that the Lord "inhabits the praises" of His people. Many times we've discovered that praise will bring the presence of God into our hearts in a blessed manner. When clouds of depression hang low, praise will drive them away. The famous English evangelist, Smith Wigglesworth, used to say, "If it's a blue Monday, lie in bed a few minutes praising the Lord."

Yes, we have abundant reasons for praising the Lord. We can praise Him for the natural blessings, for life, for health, for strength, even for the ability to work. One person said, "I complained because I had to get up early, until one morning I couldn't get up."

We should praise the Lord for the food we eat. Jesus set an example for us in offering thanks before eating. Millions of people, especially in other parts of the world, went to bed hungry last night, had nothing to eat this morning, and will go to bed hungry tonight.

We should praise the Lord for spiritual blessings. Think of the wonder of salvation—eternal life—and all it means to be truly saved from sin and hell. Then think of the wonderful baptism of the Spirit. Yes, and the refreshings that come from the Lord, and His manifest presence in our souls! How blessed we are, and how we should praise the Lord continually!

5. Praise is personal. The appeal of the Bible is, "Praise the Lord." No one else can substitute for you in this choice exercise. Sinners can't praise the Lord, for they have no personal relationship with God. And lukewarm Christians won't praise the Lord, for they do not have an up-to-date fellowship with the Lord. They are like those people in the wilderness journeys of Israel who tried to keep the manna over to the next day. It did not work for them. (See Exodus 16:14-21.) And trying to exist on yesterday's blessings will not work for us.

But we should *want* to praise the Lord. We know from Scripture how very much it pleases God. *"Whoso offereth praise glorifieth me"* (Psalm 50:23). We should want to praise Him, for it is always His will that we do so (1 Thessalonians 5:18). Neither sinners nor cold Christians can truly praise the Lord, so we who walk with Him closely must praise Him often. The response it brings is so sacred and deep! Hallelujah!

6. Praise is proper. Our praise is to the Lord Himself. True praise keeps us humble before the Lord, for humility is complete dependence upon the Lord. We know that whatever blessing we have been to others, it is all of God, and He should have the

praise and glory. If we have a special gift or ability, from where did it come? Yes, it proceeded from the Lord, so the praise belongs to Him. "It is a good thing to praise the Lord."

In healing services where the power of the Lord is present to perform real miracles, we always encourage people to praise God with all their hearts, for He alone is the Divine Healer.

We take our cue also in praising the Lord from the greatest saints in the past. Praising people are the heroes of Bible exploits. After they had crossed the Red Sea, the children of Israel were led by Moses in singing a song of praise, and Miriam with her timbrel led the women in an answering chorus. David brought the ark of God to Jerusalem with shouts of praise. Solomon led Israel in praises to God at the dedication of the temple. The angels at Bethlehem let the shepherds hear their chorus of praise. In praising the Lord we will always be in good company. Praising people have always been God's greatest saints!

The twelve disciples and Mary, the mother of Jesus, employed their tongues *"continually praising and blessing God"* (Luke 24:53).

7. Praise puts us in tune with heaven. When we praise the Lord, we are actually in tune with the heavenly language. Heaven will be full of praise. Revelation 4 relates how the 24 elders fall down, casting their crowns before the throne of God, and worship the Eternal One. Revelation 5 tells us of a vast host, *"ten thousand times ten thousand, and thousands of thousands"* (verse 11), who give praise to the Lamb.

Then Revelation 7 speaks of a great multitude that gives praise to God. Those who are bothered with what some call "excessive noise" in praising the Lord in this life will have some adjustments to make in heaven. Over there the noise will be as *"the voice of a great multitude, and as the voice of many waters, and as the voice of mighty thunderings"* (Revelation 19:6). What will they say? *"Alleluia!"* (verse 6). Shouting hallelujahs down here is indeed speaking forth the wondrous heavenly language! Hallelujah! Praise the Lord!

The Psalms have been called the "Hymnbook of the Hebrews." Psalm 150, the last psalm, ends with the words, *"Let every thing that hath breath praise the LORD. Praise ye the LORD"* (verse 6).

I believe it has been divine providence that the one universal word should be *hallelujah*, which means "Praise ye the Lord."

Hallelujah living will keep you in the main line where the Holy Spirit is working His supernatural wonders. Practice the praising principle and your life will be God-pleasing and will fulfill His best and highest purposes for your life!

Questions to Ask Yourself about Praise

1. Am I a "fair-weather Christian" who praises the Lord only when all is well and my circumstances are ideal? (1 Thessalonians 5:18)

2. Does my life lack that overflowing spirit of praise that characterizes those who are rooted, grounded, and established in the faith? (Colossians 2:6-7)

3. Have I submitted myself to the Lord to be baptized in the Holy Spirit, by *"continually praising and blessing God"*? (Luke 24:53)

4. Am I a "draw-back Christian" in whom God has no pleasure, because I withhold joyful, unceasing praises to my Lord? (Hebrews 10:38)

5. Am I neglecting the thanksgiving and praise that are essential to an effective prayer life? (Philippians 4:6)

6. Do I fully comprehend that every time I offer words of praise to God, I am truly glorifying Him? (Psalm 50:23)

7. Am I experiencing the victory in spiritual warfare that can only be brought about through praise? (2 Corinthians 10:4)

> Praise unlocks heaven's portals;
> Praise causes doubts to cease;
> Praise brings precious blessings;
> Praise leaves the sweetest peace.
>
> Praise breaks all bands asunder;
> Praise sets the captives free;
> Praise lightens every burden;
> Praise is the master key.
>
> Praise changes circumstances;
> Praise establishes the heart;
> When praise becomes perpetual,
> Praise is a Holy Art.
>
> —Frances Metcalfe

I challenge you: practice the praising principle. Praise is precious. Praise is powerful. Praise is personal. Praise pleases God!

Chapter 7

The Attitude of Gratitude

Chapter 7

The Attitude of Gratitude
∽

sk yourself this question: Do I possess the attitude of gratitude? Nine out of ten people are ungrateful, practicing base ingratitude, failing to give praise and thanks to God. This is a Bible fact!

God has a warning about the consequences of losing the attitude of gratitude: *"Because that, when they knew God, they glorified him not as God, neither were thankful; but became vain in their imaginations, and their foolish heart was darkened"* (Romans 1:21). Ingratitude extinguishes the light of God in your heart. God declares ingratitude the mark of a foolish heart.

Ten lepers were miraculously cleansed by Jesus, but only one had the attitude of gratitude. (See Luke 17:11–19.) He had cried, "Jesus, Master, have mercy on us." He realized it had been mercy from the Master that had healed him. Only as you recognize that you possess God's gifts by grace and mercy can you be truly grateful with a loving, worshipful heart.

This one leper pleased Jesus with his giving of thanks. He *"glorified God"* (Luke 17:15) by his returning to give thanks. This is why it's so important. Praise, thanksgiving, and real gratitude always glorify God.

God is not the only One who benefits from our gratitude; God also blesses us abundantly as we praise Him. The early Christians were *"continually... praising and blessing God"* (Luke 24:53). This is a vital secret of their power with God.

Right now God wants to restore to you the power of praise. Try it! You will discover the source of a power undreamed of in this world. Christ has already provided for you a complete victory over sin, iniquity, sickness, and infirmity when He died on Calvary. Now apply that victory by faith. And remember: the language of faith is *praise*.

The attitude of gratitude is one that must be cultivated. *"Seven times a day do I praise thee"* (Psalm 119:164). Set aside seven times a day to praise the Lord. It will produce wonders in your soul. *"At midnight I will rise to give thanks unto thee"* (Psalm 119:62). During the first week of each month, rise at midnight to give thanks unto the Lord. I guarantee you, you will have a closer walk with Jesus than you have ever known!

Praising God and expressing gratitude to Him is one of the most important occupations of any Christian. That is why the psalmist said,

I will bless the LORD at all times: his praise shall continually be in my mouth. My soul shall make her boast in the LORD: the humble shall hear thereof, and be glad. O magnify the LORD with me, and let us exalt his name together. (Psalm 34:1–3)

Inventors have given us remarkable discoveries and inventions that have made living easier and happier. Writers have compiled many volumes of excellent literature. Singers have been gifted to hold great audiences spellbound by their talented voices. Artists with rare ability have drawn magnificent pictures, and we marvel at their work. Presidents and kings have executed some revolutionizing judgments that have changed the course of nations. But none of the world's greatest men and women have ever done anything half as great as when a child of God praises, exalts, and glorifies Jesus, the precious Son of God. No one has ever done anything so noble as to give Jesus a few minutes of glorious praise.

We were created by almighty God so that we might have fellowship and communion with Him. The psalmist told us that our utmost purpose in being created was to praise the Lord and give Him glory.

In contrast to this statement, one of the earliest sins of humanity was failure to praise the Lord.

The apostle Peter received the revelation of God's expectations of His people:

But ye are a chosen generation, a royal priesthood, an holy nation, a peculiar people; that ye should show forth the praises of him who hath called you out of darkness into his marvellous light.

(1 Peter 2:9)

The Old Testament priesthood had to offer up animal sacrifices, but we, the *"royal priesthood,"* are to offer sacrifices of praise.

> *By him therefore let us offer the sacrifice of praise to God continually, that is, the fruit of our lips giving thanks to his name.* (Hebrews 13:15)

> *And let them sacrifice the sacrifices of thanksgiving, and declare his works with rejoicing.*
> (Psalm 107:22)

David put it in these words:

> *I will offer to thee the sacrifice of thanksgiving, and will call upon the name of the LORD.*
> (Psalm 116:17)

The book of Psalms is a book that has the keynote of praise. Praise takes effort, a real determined effort. That is why praise is called a sacrifice. There are times when perhaps we don't *feel* like praising the Lord, but the Lord wants us to praise Him—yes, sacrifice a praise unto His worthy name.

To praise the Lord requires will power and boldness. For some reason the natural man rebels against praising the Lord. But as you begin to sacrifice praise and thanksgiving unto Him, the sweet presence of the Lord will flood your soul. Then it will begin to roll out spontaneously. Glory to His name!

It is not enough to say, "I praise Jesus in my heart." The Bible commands us to praise Him out loud. *"O bless our God, ye people, and make the voice of his praise to be heard"* (Palm 66:8). In Psalm 34:1, David said, *"I will bless the LORD at all times* [This reveals to us that praise is not limited to just certain times, but rather is to be done *"at all times"*]: *his praise shall continually be in my mouth."* It is the *"fruit of our lips giving thanks to his name"* (Hebrews 13:15) that He desires.

Do you have a desire to glorify the Lord? Then praise Him! Hear His Word to you: *"Whoso offereth praise glorifieth me"* (Psalm 50:23). There are many ways to glorify the Lord, but praising Him is one of the surest ways. The more we praise Him, the more we glorify Him. From our infancy until we die, we say multiplied thousands of words. But the greatest and grandest words we say are words of praise to Jesus! Hallelujah!

Often when you come before the Lord to pray and enter into His presence, it is seemingly difficult to sense His presence. Read Psalm 100:4. You may be assured of an abundant entrance into His holy presence by singing praise to Him and entering into His gates with thanksgiving, and into His courts with praise, and by being thankful to Him and blessing His name.

Praise produces a blessed refreshing from the Lord to you. You may be tired physically, but Jesus is the Resting Place to those who love and praise Him. His rest is very rich and uplifting, and it quickly renews both mind and body. (See Matthew 11:28.)

Many times I have been in a room waiting on the Lord in preparation for a service. For 15 or 30 minutes at a time, I have done nothing but praise the Lord. Oh, what glory, what a holy hush, what a heavenly atmosphere would flood that room!

When we praise and exalt and glorify Jesus, the blessing falls. The more we praise Him, the more He blesses us. Praising the Lord brings down the power to heal the sick and perform miracles. Praise brings inspiration to the yielded soul to manifest the gifts of the Spirit.

Those who have formed the habit of praising Jesus receive wonderful answers to prayer. They not only enjoy good health, but they also have perfect peace, joy, and victory in His service. Those who praise Him often are the happiest people this side of heaven.

The best habit you can ever form is that of praising the Lord. David said,

> *Bless the LORD, O my soul: and all that is within me, bless his holy name. Bless the LORD, O my soul, and forget not all his benefits: who forgiveth all thine iniquities; who healeth all thy diseases.*
>
> (Psalm 103:1–3)

One time the country of Judah was opposed by three great armies. They cried unto the Lord, confessed their inability to cope with the dark situation, and declared, *"Our eyes are upon thee"* (2 Chronicles 20:12). In the midst of any conflict in your life, turn your eyes upon Jesus, and He will be an ever present help in the time of need. He will never leave us or forsake us (Hebrews 13:5).

Then the Spirit of the Lord spoke to the people through Jahaziel. God told them,

> *Be not afraid nor dismayed by reason of this great multitude: for the battle is not yours, but God's. To morrow go ye down against them....Ye shall not need to fight in this battle: set yourselves, stand ye still, and see the salvation of the LORD.*
>
> (2 Chronicles 20:15–17)

So instead of soldiers, the king of Judah sent a host of people to sing and praise the Lord. When they began to praise Him, those three great armies began to fight against each other—and they fought until they were completely destroyed!

The Lord will fight our battles for us even today. Let us go forth praising and glorifying His name.

In 2 Chronicles 5, we read a story of a multitude praising the Lord, and the glory of the Lord filling the temple in such a manner that the priests were unable to minister. Oftentimes we stand and praise the Lord in a service, and the glory of the Lord so fills the building that we are simply lost in Him. We can never do anything greater when we come into our services than to praise the Lord. We have too long been beggars of God; let us be praisers for what He already has done for us.

In Acts 16, we read of Paul and Silas going to Philippi to preach the Gospel. They had the reputation of being "world-upsetters." In this city, they created such a stir by casting the demon out of a woman in the name of Jesus that they were beaten and cast into jail. When they were cast into the jail, the jailer increased their punishment by making *"their feet fast in the stocks"* (verse 24).

But these two men were living dynamos for God—Spirit-filled, heaven-commissioned, with Jesus' love dwelling in their hearts. Consequently, they were not despondent and complaining about their plight. Rather, at midnight they were heard praying and singing praises to God. Then, as a result of prais-ing the Lord, another miracle was brought about, as

God sent an earthquake and opened that Philippian jail.

Before the night was over, the jailer and his family had been saved, and all the prisoners knew that the God of Paul and Silas was real.

As the poet has said, there are prisons not made with bars. Perhaps today you are in a prison of doubt and uncertainty. Or you may be in a prison of sickness and suffering. Begin to praise the Lord—sacrificing praise unto Him for His love, His tender mercies, His healing power. You will discover yourself coming into a realm of grace where faith for healing will be easily grasped and deliverance from all forms of oppression will be yours. Praise His name!

"Rejoice in the Lord alway: and again I say, Rejoice" (Philippians 4:4). There is always occasion to rejoice in Him.

I am reminded of the story of the dying man that the Cornish miner, Billy Bray, had won to Jesus. The man said, "If I had the strength, I would shout, 'Glory to God!'" Billy replied, "I would to God that ye would have shouted 'Glory to God' when ye had the strength!" Neighbor, the Lord Jesus Christ is longing to hear your heartfelt praises to Him.

"O magnify the LORD with me, and let us exalt his name together" (Psalm 34:3). Hallelujah! Hallelujah! Wonderful, wonderful Jesus! Praise His name!

A famous evangelist who had been greatly used by God suffered a severe heart attack. For many months he was restricted in what he could do physically. His doctors predicted an early, untimely death.

Many prayed for his restoration to health. But he continued to suffer from his heart ailment. Often death seemed to be seizing his life.

Then the Holy Spirit in a special visitation gave him this message: "The greatest lack in the church today is praise." The Holy Spirit caused him to realize it was not by many begging prayers that he would be healed. But the failure of his healing was caused by the failure of praise.

When the evangelist began to praise the Lord with all his might, God stretched forth His hand and healed him completely! As the Lord healed him, He gave him this message to preach everywhere he went: "Tell my people to praise Me, love Me, and give to Me."

Some may say, "The lack of holiness or separation is the greatest lack among Christians today." But when Christians truly praise the Lord, they will maintain a life of holiness unto the Lord. True praise and undedicated living just do not harmonize!

Others may say, "The lack of faith is the greatest lack among Christians." But real praise is the very language of faith, so when there is strong praise, there is strong faith being manifested.

Don't be a fair-weather Christian; that is, praising the Lord only when you feel like it or when your circumstances are ideal. God commands, *"In every thing give thanks: for this is the will of God in Christ Jesus concerning you"* (1 Thessalonians 5:18).

A well-known evangelist who has had successful campaigns in the largest churches both in Canada and the United States told me,

I have observed that the spiritual condition of a local church is gauged by their attitude toward praise. Where a real spirit of praise prevails, the spiritual condition is good. But where no genuine spirit of praise exists, carnality and worldliness run rampant among the Christians. Praise is the spiritual power that will cast out cold, dead formality in worship services. Where the people praise the Lord, great spiritual results are to be had. Souls are saved, bodies are healed, and people are baptized in the Holy Spirit. Yes, I have learned that I can soon sense the spiritual condition of a church by whether they praise the Lord or not.

If this rule applies to local churches, I believe the same rule applies to individual Christians. Your true spiritual condition is often reflected in whether you really praise the Lord or not.

A lady attending one of our services one evening whispered to me as she left the service, "Brother Gossett, I once praised the Lord like you folks do, but I've gone deeper in the Lord now, so I no longer am so demonstrative."

But when one is truly deep in the Lord, he will abound, or overflow, with thanksgiving and praise. Colossians 2:7 declares that when you are *"rooted and built up in him, and stablished in the faith,"* you will be *"abounding therein with thanksgiving."* When one goes "deeper" in the Lord, he doesn't cease praising; he praises the Lord even more!

Is the greatest lack in your life the lack of praise? If so, you are missing out on so many bountiful blessings that God bestows upon those who praise Him with joyful hearts and lips.

There was a young lady who accepted Christ as Savior, but would not follow His command to be baptized in the Holy Spirit. Of her own admission, she was halfhearted about the matter. Mainly, she objected to praise.

She testified, "I was either too shy or too stubborn to really praise the Lord. I was afraid of my own voice, it seemed, when I would hear myself speaking out words of praise to the Lord."

This holding back on abandoned praise to the Lord robbed her of receiving the mighty baptism of the Spirit. Actually, receiving the baptism is as simple as it was for the 120 people in the Upper Room. The Bible informs us that before the great event of Pentecost, they were *"continually...praising and blessing God"* (Luke 24:53).

Also, God says, *"If any man draw back, my soul will have no pleasure in him"* (Hebrews 10:38). Many have lost the fullness of God's good pleasure in their lives because they have drawn back in the matter of real praise to the Lord.

This young lady went on for some months without the baptism of the Holy Spirit. Then a near-tragedy occurred in her life. As she was walking alone on a darkened street one night, two men in a car came to an abrupt stop by the curb where she was walking. Before she fully realized what had transpired, these two men brutally grabbed her and forced her into their car. As they sped down the street and on out to the highway, the young lady was frozen with fear, wondering what would be her plight. When one of the men began to make unbecoming advances toward her, she started praying.

"Oh, one of the religious types, huh?" he mockingly said.

But she continued praying aloud to God, and the man sneeringly let her alone. As she heard the men speak, she fearfully pondered if she would ever again see her parents, her friends, and all she held dear.

She remembered God's promise, *"I will never leave thee, nor forsake thee"* (Hebrews 13:5). These words of assurance filled her heart with praise, and she began to praise the Lord with her whole heart. Her voice was filled with praises to God.

The next thing that happened that evening was totally unexpected, both by her and the kidnappers. As she was praising the Lord, suddenly she heard herself speaking in a language that she had never heard. She was speaking in an unknown tongue! Yes, right there in the back seat of that car, the Lord gloriously baptized her in the Holy Spirit!

When the men heard her speaking in tongues, one of them said, "Man, what kind of person is in this car? Listen to her speak! She's beside herself!"

With that announcement, the driver stopped the car, and they ordered the young lady out. When she got out, they demanded she turn her back to them, as they sped on down the highway.

In a short time a kind couple stopped for her and returned her to her home—safe, sound, and Spirit-filled.

This young lady had experienced an unforgettable evening. It started out to be a terrifying night of possible rape, murder, and violence. But God came on the scene mightily as this young lady praised the Lord, and He baptized her in the Holy Spirit—right there in the automobile of the men who had kidnapped her! It pays to cultivate the attitude of gratitude!

Facts about the Fruit of Our Lips

"By him therefore let us offer the sacrifice of praise to God continually, that is, the fruit of our lips giving thanks to his name" (Hebrews 13:15).

1. The test of my discipleship is to bear much fruit and glorify my Father. *"Herein is my Father glorified, that ye bear much fruit; so shall ye be my disciples"* (John 15:8).

2. Praise is the fruit that God desires to hear coming from my lips. The more I give thanks to His name, the more fruit I bear. The more fruit I bear, the more my Father is glorified! Plenty of praise produces plenty of fruit. Little praise produces little fruit. No praise produces no fruit. *"Let us offer...the fruit of our lips giving thanks to his name"* (Hebrews 13:15).

3. My words in giving thanks to Him are indeed right words; how forcible and fruitful they are! *"How forcible are right words!"* (Job 6:25).

4. Even older believers can bring forth much fruit by praising God always! *"They shall still bring forth fruit in old age"* (Psalm 92:14).

5. The Father partakes of this *"fruit of our lips"* (Hebrews 13:15) and is delighted! Praise pleases Him immensely. *"Whoso offereth praise glorifieth me"* (Psalm 50:23).

6. God promises me satisfaction with good things if I give him the fruit of my lips. *"A man shall be satisfied with good by the fruit of his mouth"* (Proverbs 12:14).

Chapter 8

One Hundred Praise Scriptures

Chapter 8

One Hundred Praise Scriptures

∞

Anyone who is serious about beginning a life of praise should fortify himself against discouragement and depression by memorizing some of the outstanding Bible passages about praise. In this chapter, you will find a list of 100 praise Scriptures that I have personally selected for your inspiration.

How to Memorize These Verses

One hundred verses might seem like a great many to commit to memory, but if you will follow this simple plan, you can do it. First, you will need 100 index cards. On each 3" x 5" card you will write the selection to be memorized, and on the reverse side, you will write the reference. After you have completed this task, you will then be ready to start your memorization program.

Memorize one verse each day, with its reference. Keep repeating the verse until you can say it without looking at the card. Learn to give the reference without turning the card over. After you have done this, then turn the card over and learn to give the verse by looking only at the reference. Each day that you add a new verse, review the previous ones.

After you have memorized four or five verses, you will proceed each day by turning all the cards with the reference side up. You should be able to recite the verse from memory the moment you see the reference. Then turn all the cards over, with the verse side up. You should be able to give the reference the moment you see the verse.

The key to this memorization program is review. As you accumulate cards and review them each day, your store of memorized verses will grow and grow.

Benefits of Memorizing These Verses

What are the benefits of memorizing these praise Scriptures? First, you will receive greater answers to prayer. Jesus said very plainly that you can receive answers to prayer only if His Word abides in you. *"If ye abide in me, and my words abide in you, ye shall ask what ye will, and it shall be done unto you"* (John 15:7).

Second, you will have greater blessings of physical health.

> *My son, attend to my words; incline thine ear unto my sayings. Let them not depart from thine eyes; keep them in the midst of thine heart. For they are life unto those that find them, and health to all their flesh.* (Proverbs 4:20–23)

Third, you will be able to wield the sword of the Spirit with greater authority. The reason Satan seeks to "brainwash" you into believing that you can't memorize these verses is this: he knows that once you are equipped with the sword of the Spirit, you will be a powerful foe. When you have the Word of God in your mind and heart, the Holy Spirit can draw upon this bank of knowledge to rout Satan at every turn. *"Take...the sword of the Spirit, which is the word of God"* (Ephesians 6:17).

Fourth, you will be able to overcome gloominess and depression. I ask all of the people who serve with me in our ministry to memorize these verses. Then I am assured that there won't be any negative, pessimistic, gloomy spirits to contend with—no sad saints dragging their feet and hindering the work of God. *"My lips shall utter praise, when thou hast taught me thy statutes"* (Psalm 119:171).

The Confession of a Victor

If you memorize one of these selections daily, it will take you a little over three months to memorize all of them. Because of the very human tendency to start well and finish poorly, I would suggest that you make the following affirmation often during your memorization program:

- ∞ I can memorize God's wonderful Word!
- ∞ God says I can—so I can!
- ∞ No matter what I think of myself, I can do it!
- ∞ Regardless of my age, I can memorize God's Word!
- ∞ In spite of past failures, I can *now* memorize God's Word!
- ∞ When it seems hard, I refuse to give up!

∞ When it appears I am slipping, I know God is helping me!

∞ *"I will not forget thy word"* (Psalm 119:16).

∞ *"I can do all things through Christ which strengtheneth me"* (Philippians 4:13).

∞ Why am I so sure? God makes me sure, that's why!

One Hundred Scriptures to Be Memorized

1. 1 Chronicles 29:13: *"Now therefore, our God, we thank thee, and praise thy glorious name."*

2. 2 Chronicles 5:13–14: *"It came even to pass, as the trumpeters and singers were as one, to make one sound to be heard in praising and thanking the* LORD; *and when they lifted up their voice with the trumpets and cymbals and instruments of music, and praised the* LORD, *saying, For he is good; for his mercy endureth forever: that then the house was filled with a cloud, even the house of the* LORD; *so that the priests could not stand to minister by reason of the cloud: for the glory of the* LORD *had filled the house of God."*

3. 2 Chronicles 20:21: *"And when he had consulted with the people, he appointed singers unto the* LORD, *and that should praise the beauty of holiness, as they went out before the army, and to say, Praise the* LORD; *for his mercy endureth for ever."*

4. Psalm 5:11: *"But let all those that put their trust in thee rejoice: let them ever shout for joy, because thou defendest them: let them also that love thy name be joyful in thee."*

5. Psalm 7:17: *"I will praise the* LORD *according to his righteousness: and will sing praise to the name of the* LORD *most high."*

6. Psalm 9:1–2: *"I will praise thee, O LORD, with my whole heart; I will show forth all thy marvellous works. I will be glad and rejoice in thee: I will sing praise to thy name, O thou most High."*

7. Psalm 9:11: *"Sing praises to the LORD, which dwelleth in Zion: declare among the people his doings."*

8. Psalm 13:6: *"I will sing unto the LORD, because he hath dealt bountifully with me."*

9. Psalm 18:3: *"I will call upon the LORD, who is worthy to be praised: so shall I be saved from mine enemies."*

10. Psalm 18:49: *"Therefore will I give thanks unto thee, O LORD, among the heathen, and sing praises unto thy name."*

11. Psalm 22:3: *"But thou art holy, O thou that inhabitest the praises of Israel."*

12. Psalm 22:22: *"I will declare thy name unto my brethren: in the midst of the congregation will I praise thee."*

13. Psalm 28:6: *"Blessed be the LORD, because he hath heard the voice of my supplications."*

14. Psalm 29:2: *"Give unto the LORD the glory due unto his name; worship the LORD in the beauty of holiness."*

15. Psalm 31:19: *"Oh how great is thy goodness, which thou hast laid up for them that fear thee; which thou hast wrought for them that trust in thee before the sons of men!"*

16. Psalm 32:11: *"Be glad in the LORD, and rejoice, ye righteous: and shout for joy, all ye that are upright in heart."*

17. Psalm 33:1: *"Rejoice in the LORD, O ye righteous: for praise is comely for the upright."*

18. Psalm 34:1: *"I will bless the LORD at all times: his praise shall continually be in my mouth."*

19. Psalm 35:18: *"I will give thee thanks in the great congregation: I will praise thee among much people."*

20. Psalm 35:27: *"Let them shout for joy, and be glad, that favour my righteous cause: yea, let them say continually, Let the LORD be magnified, which hath pleasure in the prosperity of his servant."*

21. Psalm 35:28: *"And my tongue shall speak of thy righteousness and of thy praise all the day long."*

22. Psalm 40:3: *"And he hath put a new song in my mouth, even praise unto our God: many shall see it, and fear, and shall trust in the LORD."*

23. Psalm 42:11: *"Why art thou cast down, O my soul? and why art thou disquieted within me? hope thou in God: for I shall yet praise him, who is the health of my countenance, and my God."*

24. Psalm 44:8: *"In God we boast all the day long, and praise thy name for ever."*

25. Psalm 47:1: *"O clap your hands, all ye people; shout unto God with the voice of triumph."*

26. Psalm 47:6: *"Sing praises to God, sing praises: sing praises unto our King, sing praises."*

27. Psalm 48:1: *"Great is the LORD, and greatly to be praised in the city of our God, in the mountain of his holiness."*

28. Psalm 50:14: *"Offer unto God thanksgiving; and pay thy vows unto the most High."*

29. Psalm 50:23: *"Whoso offereth praise glorifieth me: and to him that ordereth his conversation aright will I show the salvation of God."*

30. Psalm 51:15: *"O Lord, open thou my lips; and my mouth shall show forth thy praise."*

31. Psalm 52:9: *"I will praise thee for ever, because thou hast done it: and I will wait on thy name; for it is good before thy saints."*

32. Psalm 54:6: *"I will freely sacrifice unto thee: I will praise thy name, 0 Lord; for it is good."*

33. Psalm 56:4: *"In God I will praise his word, in God I have put my trust; I will not fear what flesh can do unto me."*

34. Psalm 56:10: *"In God will I praise his word: in the Lord will I praise his word."*

35. Psalm 56:12: *"Thy vows are upon me, O God: I will render praises unto thee."*

36. Psalm 57:7: *"My heart is fixed, O God, my heart is fixed: I will sing and give praise."*

37. Psalm 57:9: *"I will praise thee, O Lord, among the people: I will sing unto thee among the nations."*

38. Psalm 63:3: *"Because thy lovingkindness is better than life, my lips shall praise thee."*

39. Psalm 63:4: *"Thus will I bless thee while I live: I will lift up my hands in thy name."*

40. Psalm 63:5: *"My soul shall be satisfied as with marrow and fatness; and my mouth shall praise thee with joyful lips."*

41. Psalm 66:2: *"Sing forth the honour of his name: make his praise glorious."*

42. Psalm 66:8: *"O bless our God, ye people, and make the voice of his praise to be heard."*

43. Psalm 67:3: *"Let the people praise thee, O God; let all the people praise thee."*

44. Psalm 68:19: *"Blessed be the Lord, who daily loadeth us with benefits, even the God of our salvation."*

45. Psalm 69:30: *"I will praise the name of God with a song, and will magnify him with thanksgiving."*

46. Psalm 71:8: *"Let my mouth be filled with thy praise and with thy honour all the day."*

47. Psalm 71:14: *"But I will hope continually, and will yet praise thee more and more."*

48. Psalm 74:21: *"O let not the oppressed return ashamed: let the poor and needy praise thy name."*

49. Psalm 79:13: *"So we thy people and sheep of thy pasture will give thee thanks for ever: we will show forth thy praise to all generations."*

50. Psalm 86:10: *"For thou art great, and doest wondrous things: thou art God alone."*

51. Psalm 92:1: *"It is a good thing to give thanks unto the Lord, and to sing praises unto thy name, O most High."*

52. Psalm 95:1–2: *"O come, let us sing unto the Lord: let us make a joyful noise to the rock of our salvation. Let us come before his presence with thanksgiving, and make a joyful noise unto him with psalms."*

53. Psalm 100:1–4: *"Make a joyful noise unto the Lord, all ye lands. Serve the Lord with gladness: come before his presence with singing. Know ye that the Lord he is God: it is he that hath made us, and not we ourselves; we are his people, and the sheep of his pasture. Enter into his*

gates with thanksgiving, and into his courts with praise: be thankful unto him, and bless his name."

54. Psalm 103:1–2: *"Bless the LORD, O my soul: and all that is within me, bless his holy name. Bless the LORD, O my soul, and forget not all his benefits."*

55. Psalm 105:1–2: *"O give thanks unto the LORD; call upon his name: make known his deeds among the people. Sing unto him, sing psalms unto him: talk ye of all his wondrous works."*

56. Psalm 106:2: *"Who can utter the mighty acts of the LORD? who can show forth all his praise?"*

57. Psalm 106:12: *"Then believed they his words; they sang his praise."*

58. Psalm 107:8: *"Oh that men would praise the LORD for his goodness, and for his wonderful works to the children of men!"*

59. Psalm 113:3: *"From the rising of the sun unto the going down of the same the Lord's name is to be praised."*

60. Psalm 116:17: *"I will offer to thee the sacrifice of thanksgiving, and will call upon the name of the LORD."*

61. Psalm 119:171: *"My lips shall utter praise, when thou hast taught me thy statutes."*

62. Psalm 134:2: *"Lift up your hands in the sanctuary, and bless the LORD."*

63. Psalm 138:1: *"I will praise thee with my whole heart: before the gods will I sing praise unto thee."*

64. Psalm 145:1–3: *"I will extol thee, my God, O king; and I will bless thy name for ever and ever. Every day will I bless thee; and I will praise thy name for ever and ever. Great is the LORD, and greatly to be praised; and his greatness is unsearchable."*

65. Psalm 145:21: *"My mouth shall speak the praise of the* Lord: *and let all flesh bless his holy name for ever and ever."*

66. Psalm 147:1: *"Praise ye the* Lord: *for it is good to sing praises unto our God; for it is pleasant; and praise is comely."*

67. Psalm 147:7: *"Sing unto the* Lord *with thanksgiving; sing praise upon the harp unto our God."*

68. Psalm 149:1: *"Praise ye the* Lord. *Sing unto the* Lord *a new song, and his praise in the congregation of saints."*

69. Psalm 150:1–2: *"Praise ye the* Lord. *Praise God in his sanctuary: praise him in the firmament of his power. Praise him for his mighty acts: praise him according to his excellent greatness."*

70. Psalm 150:6: *"Let every thing that hath breath praise the* Lord. *Praise ye the* Lord."

71. Isaiah 25:1: *"O* Lord, *thou art my God; I will exalt thee, I will praise thy name; for thou hast done wonderful things; thy counsels of old are faithfulness and truth."*

72. Jonah 2:9: *"But I will sacrifice unto thee with the voice of thanksgiving; I will pay that that I have vowed. Salvation is of the* Lord."

73. Luke 17:15–16: *"And one of them, when he saw that he was healed, turned back, and with a loud voice glorified God, and fell down on his face at his feet, giving him thanks: and he was a Samaritan."*

74. Luke 18:43: *"And immediately he received his sight, and followed him, glorifying God: and all the people, when they saw it, gave praise unto God."*

75. Luke 19:37–38: *"And when he was come nigh, even now at the descent of the mount of Olives, the whole multitude of the disciples began to rejoice and praise God with a loud voice for all the mighty works that they had seen; saying, Blessed be the King that cometh in the name of the Lord: peace in heaven, and glory in the highest."*

76. Luke 24:53: *"And [they] were continually in the temple, praising and blessing God."*

77. Acts 2:46–47: *"And they, continuing daily with one accord in the temple, and breaking bread from house to house, did eat their meat with gladness and singleness of heart, praising God, and having favour with all the people. And the Lord added to the church daily such as should be saved."*

78. Acts 3:8: *"And he leaping up stood, and walked, and entered with them into the temple, walking, and leaping, and praising God."*

79. Acts 16:25: *"And at midnight Paul and Silas prayed, and sang praises unto God: and the prisoners heard them."*

80. 1 Corinthians 14:15–16: *"What is it then? I will pray with the spirit, and I will pray with the understanding also: I will sing with the spirit, and I will sing with the understanding also. Else when thou shalt bless with the spirit, how shall he that occupieth the room of the unlearned say Amen at thy giving of thanks, seeing he understandeth not what thou sayest?"*

81. 1 Corinthians 15:57: *"But thanks be to God which giveth us the victory through our Lord Jesus Christ."*

82. 2 Corinthians 2:14: *"Now thanks be unto God, which always causeth us to triumph in Christ, and maketh*

manifest the savour of his knowledge by us in every place."

83. 2 Corinthians 9:15: *"Thanks be unto God for his unspeakable gift."*

84. 2 Corinthians 10:17: *"But he that glorieth, let him glory in the Lord."*

85. Ephesians 5:4: *"Neither filthiness, nor foolish talking, nor jesting, which are not convenient: but rather giving of thanks."*

86. Ephesians 5:19–20: *"Speaking to yourselves in psalms and hymns and spiritual songs, singing and making melody in your heart to the Lord; giving thanks always for all things unto God and the Father in the name of our Lord Jesus Christ."*

87. Philippians 4:4: *"Rejoice in the Lord alway: and again I say, Rejoice."*

88. Philippians 4:6: *"Be careful for nothing; but in every thing by prayer and supplication with thanksgiving let your requests be made known unto God."*

89. Colossians 1:12: *"Giving thanks unto the Father, which hath made us meet to be partakers of the inheritance of the saints in light."*

90. Colossians 2:7: *"Rooted and built up in him, and stablished in the faith, as ye have been taught, abounding therein with thanksgiving."*

91. Colossians 3:15: *"And let the peace of God rule in your hearts, to the which also ye are called in one body; and be ye thankful."*

92. Colossians 4:2: *"Continue in prayer, and watch in the same with thanksgiving."*

93. 1 Thessalonians 5:18: *"In every thing give thanks: for this is the will of God in Christ Jesus concerning you."*

94. 1 Timothy 4:4: *"For every creature of God is good, and nothing to be refused, if it be received with thanksgiving."*

95. 2 Timothy 3:1–2: *"In the last days perilous times shall come. For men shall be...unthankful."*

96. Hebrews 13:15: *"By him therefore let us offer the sacrifice of praise to God continually, that is, the fruit of our lips giving thanks to his name."*

97. 1 Peter 2:9: *"But ye are a chosen generation, a royal priesthood, an holy nation, a peculiar people; that ye should show forth the praises of him who hath called you out of darkness into his marvellous light."*

98. 1 Peter 4:11: *"If any man speak, let him speak as the oracles of God; if any man minister, let him do it as of the ability which God giveth: that God in all things may be glorified through Jesus Christ, to whom be praise and dominion for ever and ever. Amen."*

99. Revelation 19:1: *"And after these things I heard a great voice of much people in heaven, saying, Alleluia; salvation, and glory, and honour, and power, unto the Lord our God."*

100. Revelation 19:5: *"And a voice came out of the throne, saying, Praise our God, all ye his servants, and ye that fear him, both small and great."*

Chapter 9

Hallelujah Living

∞

Chapter 9

Hallelujah Living

∽

A few years ago I was in a campaign with Pastor A. E. Wunder, a real man of the Spirit. Our crusade received newspaper publicity; the editor said it was only right that the people of his city should know what the Lord was doing for the people, especially the healing miracles.

One day Brother Wunder was led by God to go down the coast to take food to a young pastor and his family, who had opened a pioneer work in an unevangelized area.

When he got to their home, he heard them praying. He listened for a moment when he stepped onto the front porch. The young wife was praying for food!

Since Brother Wunder was well-armed with boxes of food, he simply burst through the front door and exclaimed, "You can get up, folks; the answer has come. I've brought the food."

The family arose and rejoiced that God had indeed answered their prayers.

While the young wife was preparing the food, Brother Wunder noticed that she looked very depressed when she walked by the refrigerator.

"Sister," he said, "you seem depressed every time you walk by that fridge. Why is that?"

"I wasn't aware that I looked depressed," she replied, "but it must be because that thing has been empty so often when I needed food for my children."

Brother Wunder felt led by God to throw down a challenge to her faith. "Sister, I believe if you will shout *hallelujah* at that refrigerator every time you walk past it, God will respond and fill up that refrigerator, and He'll keep it filled for you."

The young wife looked at him in amazement. It sounded ridiculous.

Brother Wunder countered, "It seemed foolish for the Israelites to march around Jericho and shout to see those walls fall down. But they shouted anyway, and down the walls came. It seemed ridiculous for Jehoshaphat to have the singers and praisers lead the way singing and praising in the face of three great armies. But God was pleased and brought them great victory and deliverance that day. It was a strange thing for Paul and Silas to be praising God at midnight in that filthy old jail, but God responded and sent the earthquake and freedom. So, Sister, I believe God will meet you if you will say *hallelujah* every time you walk by the refrigerator!"

The lady respected Brother Wunder as a real man of God, so she started quietly saying *hallelujah* every time she walked by the fridge. In a short time, the blessing of this experience was so abundant that she was fairly shouting it out: *"Hallelujah!"*

A few days later, Brother Wunder returned to see how things were going. The young couple saw him arrive, and they met him on the porch with a couple of healthy hallelujahs.

Then the wife told him a story. "I kept on shouting *hallelujah* every time I walked past the refrigerator. And the Lord moved upon an unsaved man in this town to bring us all of the frozen meats, foods, and things we could get in the fridge. It is just bulging at the seams."

Months later, I saw Brother Wunder again and asked how the young pastor and his family were getting along.

"I saw them recently," Pastor Wunder said. "The young wife is still praising God and shouting *hallelujah* at the refrigerator, and God is keeping it filled!"

That is bold faith. I am sold on being bold, even in praising God. Bold praising evidences bold faith.

I have related this account on different occasions. It has inspired others to begin shouting *hallelujah* at their barriers and obstacles.

A man in Tulsa without employment had gone to a certain plant several times and was always turned away.

Of his own accord he took up this challenge of God. The next time he went to this plant, he stood outside the gate and shouted softly, *"Hallelujah!"* Then he walked into the office. Sure enough he was hired that day!

In Regina, Saskatchewan, a young married man heard this same account. He had been unable to secure a job at his trade. Daily, he had gone to the labor office but always met the same reply: "No openings."

Courageously he told his wife, "After hearing Brother Gossett relate that experience about the power of praise, I'm going to stop before I go into that office, and shout a few *hallelujahs*. I believe God will see to it that I have a job."

He did just that, and when he walked into the office, the phone rang. The man at the desk, answering the phone, suddenly motioned to my friend. "I just now have a call for your trade. Can you go to work today?" Praise God, my friend went to work *that day!*

Is there something magical about the word *hallelujah?* Certainly not. But God does respond to faith. Shouting *hallelujah* or praising Him in other ways shows our genuine faith in His loving provision.

The Lord *"inhabitest the praises of Israel"* (Psalm 22:3). God lives in and dwells in our bold praises, and He manifests Himself in response to them.

When it comes to praising God, I am sold on being bold. We can shout *hallelujahs* right in the face of adversity, illness, discouragement, and needs. I've tried it, and I know it works!

Five Reasons for Lifting the Hands in Praise

One of the ways we can praise God boldly is by lifting our hands to Him. Although this particular expression of worship may seem somewhat strange to some, there is plenty of biblical basis for the practice. Here are five reasons why we ought to lift our hands in praise:

1. Lifting the hands is a scriptural way of expressing thanks to God: *"Because thy lovingkindness is better than life, my lips shall praise thee. Thus will I bless thee while I live: I will lift up my hands in thy name"* (Psalm 63:3–4).

2. Lifting the hands is an appropriate way to worship God in the sanctuary. I know that in public worship, all things are to be done *"decently and in order"* (1 Corinthians 14:40); but there is nothing disorderly about praising Jesus in the sanctuary by lifting up my hands! *"Lift up your hands in the sanctuary, and bless the LORD"* (Psalm 134:2).

3. It is God's will that we worship in this way. Man's order in religion is often ceremonial, ritualistic, and after human tradition. But God's order in worship is life, liberty, and lifting up of hands! *"I will therefore that men pray every where, lifting up holy hands, without wrath and doubting"* (1 Timothy 2:8).

4. Lifting the hands is a symbolic way of expressing ascending worship: *"Let my prayer be set forth before thee as incense; and the lifting up of my hands as the evening sacrifice"* (Psalm 141:2).

5. Lifting the hands is a way of expressing spiritual thirsting: *"I stretch forth my hands unto thee: my soul thirsteth after thee, as a thirsty land"* (Psalm 143:6).

Chapter 10

Adventures in Praise

Adventures in Praise

∞

*D*oes this life of praise really work? Well, the proof of the pudding is in the eating! Here are several testimonies from friends who have embarked on a life of praise and have found it gloriously practical.

The first report comes from Patricia C. Eskin of Havertown, Pennsylvania:

It is one of those days known as "one of those days." It has been pouring steadily all day, and the cellar is flooded. My hair, which I washed and set this morning, is hanging in strings about my face. At work, I dropped my papers at least four times and made several errors.

When I came home from shopping, I found I had the wrong kind of bread. The cake I baked did not rise properly. Bills have come in today that I do not know how to pay. The rice burned while I was trying to rearrange things in the wet cellar below.

Then, all of a sudden, "Praise You, Lord!" began chiming in my mind. "Praise You, dear Lord; praise You, Father! I know You are sovereign, and somewhere else at this moment Your goodness and lovingkindness are being felt by someone anew. Praise You, Lord!"

And in this wonderful moment of praise, the grumbling inside me stopped. I was happy, and all was well.

So it is every time of late when things are going wrong and getting me down; praise puts a new face on everything!

Do you believe that Holy Spirit power caused Peter's nighttime fishing experience to be transformed from dismal failure to overwhelming success? Again, do you believe it was the power of the Spirit that caused the coins to be formed in the fish's mouth, whereby Peter and the Master could pay their taxes? Then is it possible that Holy Spirit power could cause a woman to have success in fishing, where before she had been completely a failure? If you are a Bible believer, I'm convinced you can readily believe all of these things. Mrs. Norma Nichols of Freeland, Washington, is the wife of a businessman in that city. She shares with us a beautiful account of an example of childlike faith in God's goodness and provision:

I want to tell you how your book made a "hallelujah fisherwoman" out of me. For the past three years I have hiked with my husband deep into the mountains to fish the mountain streams and have waded up and down from waterfall to waterfall, pool to pool. Sounds pretty good, doesn't it? I thought so, too, except for one thing: not once in three years did I catch a fish that I could keep (one that was over the required six inches), although my husband almost always caught fish.

On our last fishing trip of this season, my husband was gathering up our fishing gear, and I was packing food for the hike. I mentioned to my husband that I thought there must be something wrong with my fishing gear since, after three years of trying, I had caught nothing. All my husband said was, "I think you are complaining a lot." But it rang a bell. Grumble Street? Well, why not start living on Thanksgiving Street?

On our long hike I dragged further behind than usual. I had to get some practice in praising God out loud. I started out saying, "Hallelujah! Praise God in the name of the Lord Jesus! Thank You, Lord Jesus!" I prayed out loud and asked the Lord to make me a real hallelujah Christian that very day—a hallelujah fisherwoman!

I stepped over to the creek and said, "Lord, here is my hook; You put the fish on it, and I will pull it out and give You the praise for it." I was so anxious to see what the Lord would do that I didn't wait to find a good hole, but tossed it into the shallow, rushing water. No sooner had my fly hit the water than, praise God, a nine-inch rainbow trout took my hook! I pulled it out and gave God the thanks and praise.

I walked downstream a little and perched on a log, dropping my flies down into the pool. As soon as my flies sank below the surface of the water, the pool began to boil with fish. Praise God! The fish were actually fighting over my hooks! I caught one that was nearly twelve inches long. He was so fat and heavy that I was afraid my pole wouldn't take it.

Praise the Lord for this small thing. I know that it must have been a small thing to Him. I felt that He was laughing and playing with me. This to me was so much more than the fish, that our God was even playing with me. His beauty humbles me. How wonderful He is! Glory to God! This was a wonderful witness to my husband. After many hours of fishing that morning, when he had still caught nothing, he said, "You know, if you hadn't caught those two big ones, I would have said that there weren't any fish in there!" Hallelujah!

Mrs. Jane Terry of Orlando, Florida, has a beautiful testimony of a recent event in her life:

This morning I went to the kitchen to fix breakfast. When I opened the freezer to get the orange juice, everything was defrosted! I laid my hands on the freezer and prayed out loud. My two children came in and watched with interest, curious as to what my reaction would be to this "major catastrophe."

At the breakfast table we thanked God, praised Him, and rested.

Later, such thoughts entered my mind as "You need a new freezer. Sell the car for cash to pay for a new freezer. Go to the neighbor's and ask her to phone the repair man. Go to the store and buy a freezer on credit." With each thought, a headache came. I prayed that if it was God's will for me to sell the car and get a new freezer, He'd tell me where to go. So I got dressed and continued to thank and praise God out loud. Later, I read Psalms 26 through 30 out loud and praised God with uplifted hands, really adoring Him and being so thankful, knowing I have the victory of Jesus Christ whether a situation looks good or bad.

I was just about to leave when the Lord suggested that I check the freezer. So I did. It was working beautifully! Praise the Lord!

Often it is necessary to stand firmly against the Adversary in Jesus' name, as well as entering into praise for the victory of our Lord. Mrs. Pat Cruse of Renton, Washington, is one who has experienced a twofold victory in spiritual activity. She has perceived the source of her opposition to be satanic. As she states it, "I rebuke Satan and praise God." Wise is the Christian who discerns his trouble to be satanic and then employs the power of praise against the Devil. Here is her account:

One day the back of my head began to throb near the neck. I had several hours to work, and then I was to meet my relatives at the airport. By the time I arrived at the airport, I had a splitting headache.

I had, by turns, rebuked Satan and praised God. All the while, the pain continued to increase slowly in intensity, bringing periods of nausea. The pain throbbed on with great viciousness, and I became almost unable to drive home, but the Lord was my traveling Companion.

Upon arriving home I called my church, and a dear brother, together with the pastor and assistant pastor, agreed for my healing. Back with even more fury came relentless pain. I became enraged at Satan and his brazen attack even after I had claimed my healing. I got out Brother Gossett's helps on praise and began to read them. I didn't read them quietly or inaudibly, I read them so loud, the walls echoed my claims. This was very painful—with all that noise and effort! I raised my hands and sang loudly, "Set My Spirit Free That I May Worship Thee," "Hallelujah," and "I Shall Praise the Lord at All Times." The sharp edge of pain went away. Hallelujah! More pain began fading, until the last dull twinge was absent and my praises had turned into "Thank You, thank You, Jesus!" God inhabited my praises and brought a healing. Praise God! His mercy endures forever!

My broadcast opens each day with the singing of the "Hallelujah Chorus." How does that beautiful piece of music affect you? Miss Ruth Weber of Red Deer, Alberta, states, "I almost jump for joy when I hear your broadcast and they sing that 'Hallelujah Chorus.'" Miss Weber has a reason for such jubilation, for the message of praise has transformed her whole life. I'll let her tell about it:

Here is a very precious experience that has challenged me to trust God at all times in all events:

Your writings on praise started me on a road that I barely knew anything about. Now I am reminded to give thanks and praise to God in everything, good or otherwise, and tell what He is teaching me. He teaches me so much in such a simple way. Praise His name!

One of my challenging experiences happened while I was on vacation this summer visiting my brothers and sisters in Ontario. When I went to the Union Station in Toronto, I found I had two and a half hours before my train left. I was alone, just waiting, when I opened my purse and couldn't find my wallet. I knew where I had left it: at a hotel telephone booth, where I had made a call. My mind panicked but my heart was praising God— something completely new to me. I was learning to praise in all circumstances.

I thought about having no money and about my credit cards, ownership card, and license—all in my wallet. Still this praise continued. I went back to the hotel and found my wallet safe with the security police of that hotel. When I thanked them, they said, "Don't thank us. It was a guest of the hotel who turned it in, and he has left."

I thank God continually for an experience like that. When I asked God what He was trying to teach me, immediately the thought came, "Trust Me; I'll take care of you." How I praise Him for this experience! It has strengthened my faith to trust Him more.

Some friends suggested later that I only praised God because it turned out all right. But, praise God, I can tell them praise was there from the beginning, even when I had no assurance that I'd ever see my wallet again. *"In every thing give thanks: for this is the will of God"* (1 Thessalonians 5:18).

One of the great songs of the Spirit being sung these days declares, "All over the world, the Spirit of the Lord is moving!" Testimonies come to my office from people on various continents sharing what the Lord is doing through our ministry and the message of praise. The Word of God is the basis of our presenting the praising principle, the Holy Spirit is the Teacher, and Jesus must have all the praise and glory for what is being done. Mrs. Linda J. Dunford, who is stationed with her husband in Germany in the U. S. Army, shares how she put the praising principle into practice:

The Lord is constantly doing things for us, and where to begin and where to end would be a problem—so I will share a happening about the power and victory over the powers of darkness that is in the lovely name of Jesus.

During the winter, one Saturday, my husband was preparing to go to Oberammergau (Bavaria), Germany, for a week of school to which the U.S. Army was sending him. As he loves to ski but finds few opportunities to do so, we had decided that he should leave early on the Saturday before classes began and ski during the weekend. He also planned to use that time for a mini-retreat with the Lord.

We arose early and packed the car. Then the trouble began. First a problem with the furnace, then a problem with a radiator in the house; the German landlord came to see what he could do. Then the car engine started racing, and when the accelerator was depressed, the engine lost power. All these things took time to work on, and it began to get late.

Two o'clock in the afternoon came. The furnace worked, the radiator was fine, but not the car. It is a seven-hour trip from where we live to Oberammergau. My husband said that he was going to take the car to the garage. I was getting cold, so I went in and began cleaning up the kitchen. As I did, I became angry to think that the Devil was trying to stop my husband from going on his weekend. So I yelled, "You evil spirits, in the name of Jesus Christ, I command you to take your hands off that car and stop keeping my husband from going on his mini-retreat!" I heard a little voice say, "Hee, hee, it won't work." So I replied, "Hee, hee yourself, Devil, it will work because it's in the name of Jesus, and you have to obey." Less than five minutes later, my husband came in and said, "I'm going now." I answered, "To the garage?" And he replied, "No, to Oberammergau; the car is working fine now."

There is wonderful power in His name, and how we praised Him for victory! Sometimes the Lord amazes me as to what He will do as we step out for Him in faith.

What do you do when you receive a phone call after midnight informing you that your son's life has ended in an accident? This very experience happened for Mrs. Jean King of South Edmonton, Alberta, in the summer of 1971. Immediately the Spirit of the Lord brought to her this Scripture: *"I will trust, and not be afraid"* (Isaiah 12:2). Again the Holy Spirit brought her another Scripture: *"Blessed is the man that feareth the* LORD, *that delighteth greatly in his commandments....He shall not be afraid of evil tidings: his heart is fixed, trusting in the* LORD" (Psalm 112:1, 7).

These wonderful Scriptures assured Mrs. King that she did not have to be afraid of evil tidings, for her heart was fixed, trusting in the Lord.

The normal reaction of a mother who has just been informed by an emergency phone call that her son has been killed would be to panic. But this is what Mrs. King did:

> I fell on my knees and said this Scripture: *"I will trust, and not be afraid"* (Isaiah 12:2). I just couldn't say anything else. The Holy Spirit helped me just praise God for almost an hour.
>
> What had happened? My son, Larry, had been in this awful accident on his motorcycle going down the highway at eleven o'clock at night. It was raining so hard that he and his friends had to stop in a garage to wait until the rain let up a bit; then they started out again, little knowing a car was stalled in the middle of the highway a short distance ahead with no warning or signal lights whatsoever. My son was in the middle of the road with his motorcycle, his friends on each side of him. His friends had enough room to swerve and miss the car, but my son hit it at 60 miles

per hour. He knocked the car ahead 35 feet with the impact of his body and his bike. He had his jaw broken in three places, some teeth knocked out, his ankle fractured, and a fractured skull.

Earlier that same evening, the Spirit of the Lord had warned me that Larry needed my prayers for protection. Then about midnight, my daughter came telling me that Larry's friends had phoned that his life had ended when he hit the car. At the hospital, Larry's heart had quit beating, but the doctors and nurses worked on him and gave him some adrenaline, and it started up again. Little did I realize this, as the Spirit of God kept me praising Him. No wonder God says He inhabits the praises of His people (Psalm 22:3).

You can imagine my joy when I learned Larry was still alive! He was in the hospital at Edson, but God knew it would be hard for me to go there, so again He worked a miracle by sending Larry to Edmonton. They didn't have the proper equipment to work on Larry in the Edson Hospital. Every day, as my husband and I went to the hospital to see him, the Lord just kept my faith strong in praising Him, and each time we'd see such an improvement in him. Within a week he was home and mended fine!

I'm happy to say the Lord just took over and helped me to keep praising Him while He worked it all out. Isn't the Lord wonderful?

I am so thankful that the Lord indeed inhabited my praises on behalf of my son, brought him back to life, and made him completely whole within one week!

Until recently, the medical profession stated that a human body could not survive with burned areas covering more than 40 percent of the body. But here we have the testimony of Mr. George Godkin of Turner Valley, Alberta, who received deep, extensive burns on over 65 percent of his body. As a matter of fact, even his ears were completely burned off. As he learned how Peter, Paul, and others were able to praise the Lord while in prison, with their backs cut to ribbons by the lash, Mr. Godkin, too, launched out in faith for his own need:

> On January 7, 1948, there developed a break in the gas line coming into our house, causing raw gas to pour into the kitchen, which ignited from the kitchen stove. I was in the basement at the time of the explosion and was forced to run through the fire in the kitchen to get out of the house. Upon my arriving outside, my wife said that our six-week-old daughter was still in there. I rushed back into the inferno and carried her out.
>
> The result of all these trips through the fire was that I received deep, extensive bums to over 65 percent of my body. Even my ears were completely burned off. At that time the medical profession claimed that a human body could not survive with burned areas covering more than 40 percent of the body. However, our gracious Lord saw fit to save my soul, to give me a fantastic trip into the spiritual realm, and to teach me how to endure physical pain by praising Him.
>
> For a short time the two doctors on my case fed me drugs to ease the terrific pain of

my burned body. However, it was after the drugs had been discontinued that our Lord taught me how to endure physical pain by praising Him. This is not sensible or reasonable to the human mind, but if Christians would only put into practice the habit of praising our Lord when physical pain strikes, they would find the intense physical pain would be eased as they praise God.

I can now understand how Peter, Paul, and others were able to praise the Lord while in prison with their backs cut to ribbons by the lash. My wife has watched me twist in physical pain while all the time I was praising the Lord. I kept telling her how the intense physical pain always eased up as I praised God. But of course the human mind cannot accept this, so one must put into practice the art of praising the Lord during a tribulation period, whether it be physical pain, accident, or a death in the family.

I have developed the habit of praising God in everything. I know when death comes to this earthly body of mine, I will leave this world praising our Lord because I have developed the praising habit over the years.

Sorrow comes and visits all of our lives. Is praise a Christian reaction to the loss of a dear loved one? Mrs. Mary Flower of Chilliwack, British Columbia, and Mrs. Margaret Foster of North Wilkesboro, North Carolina, both share their experiences in the loss of dear loved ones and how praise to God has been a source of great comfort and a Spirit-given therapy in the adjustment of their bereavements.

Mrs. Flower writes,

I am glad to share my testimony of victory through praise. The victories have been at times without number, and I am so glad. Sometimes when I praise the Lord for half an hour at a time, I've experienced wonderful cleansing, refreshing, and healing. The great thrill to me is that the Word of God is so faithful and true, giving us assurance that the Lord does dwell in our heartfelt praises. If I build Him a praise house, it attracts His attention, and He honors His Word and comes in. Hallelujah!

I was fully convinced of this in the time of bereavement when my dear mother went home to glory. In the natural realm I would have been greatly depressed and full of sorrow; but I'd heard the message of praise and how it brings deliverance, so I started to praise Him and kept on until I got over that deep valley of sorrow. All the time I praised Him, I had on the garment of praise in place of the spirit of heaviness.

Also, when my only daughter passed away, it could have been a very deep sorrow; but as I sat in that funeral parlor, the rain of His presence came down on me, and I could have laughed with joy!

The Lord is so sweet and precious, and He loves to shower His glory on those who are truly His born-again, Spirit-filled, worshipping children. *"Thanks be to God, which giveth us the victory through our Lord Jesus Christ"* (1 Corinthians 15:57).

I also know how the Adversary (Satan) hates to hear us praising Jesus. But I've known the powers of darkness to be driven out by praising and extolling Jesus. To Him be all the glory. Amen.

Mrs. Foster writes,

I have learned in the last year just how much God wants our praises. I have learned to give thanks in everything, for this is the will of God in Christ Jesus concerning *me*. This morning I awakened, realizing this was "her" day—the birthday of our lovely daughter, who, with our precious son, had been killed in an automobile accident several years before.

As I went to the window and drew open the curtain, the sun was coming through the trees, shining with brilliance against the beautifully colored leaves. Over the sound waves of the radio came the melody, "Beautiful Isle of Somewhere." "God lives, and all is well," the words came to me—and at that time the glory of almighty God filled the room. Never have I felt the joy and peace that I knew at that moment.

"Gail and David are alive with Jesus," I said. Then I raised my hands in praise. "Praise You, Jesus; praise You that my children are there with You. Praise You that You know what is best for me and for them. Praise You that You gave Your life for us so that we might live forever. Praise You! Praise You!"

So you see, there's power in praise! Praising God for everything is the key to a happy, victorious

Christian life. William Law wrote this formula for happiness:

> The shortest, surest way to all happiness is this: Make it a rule to thank and praise God for everything that happens to you, for it is certain that, whatever seeming calamity comes to you, if you thank and praise God for it, you turn it into a blessing. If you could, therefore, work miracles, you could not do more for yourself than by this thankful spirit, for it needs not a word spoken, and it turns all that it touches into happiness.

Do you thank God for the unpleasant things as well as the pleasant things that come your way? Complaining will drag you down into the darkness of despondency. Praise will lift you into the glorious light of God's presence. Do not smile and say, "I'm not doing too bad under the circumstances"—when praise can lift you above the circumstances!

When the psalmist David did not see a very pleasant present, he thanked God for the blessings of the past. Have you praised God recently for all His past benefits?

There's power in praise! Therefore, obey the biblical command, *"In every thing give thanks"* (1 Thessalonians 5:18).

You have the power to decide whether you will be a grumbling, defeated Christian or a praising, triumphant Christian. You must make the decision! O friend, decide to praise God for everything, pleasant or unpleasant. Begin a life of praise, and begin it *now.*

Praise the Lord Anyhow!

"His praise shall continually be in my mouth" (Psalm 34:1). The following are seven reasons why we ought to praise the Lord, whether our circumstances are good or bad.

1. Do you feel the joy of the Lord in your soul? Praise the Lord! Or do you feel blank inside, or even worse, do you feel depressed? Praise the Lord anyhow! It is *"the sacrifice of praise to God continually"* that you are commanded to offer (Hebrews 13:15). *"The sacrifice of praise"* means "praise the Lord anyhow, especially when you don't feel like it!"

2. Are all your children saved? Praise the Lord! Or are some still wandering in sin? Praise the Lord anyhow! God promises you that, by believing, *all* your household will be saved (Acts 16:31). Praising the Lord for their salvation in advance of seeing them in the fold is evidence that you truly believe!

3. Are all your bills paid up-to-date? Praise the Lord! Or are you plagued by financial problems? Praise the Lord anyhow! Praise activates God's promise of plenty of money to supply all your needs. Praise Him as you affirm, "My God is *now* supplying all my needs." (See Philippians 4:19.) Repeat it seven times. Then say, "Thank You, Father for Your riches now."

4. Are you enjoying good health? Praise the Lord! Or are you having health problems? Praise the Lord anyhow! Healing is received by faith, and praise is the language of faith. *"As thou hast believed, so be it done unto thee"* (Matthew 8:13).

5. Is the weather good, and to your liking? Praise the Lord! Or is it unpleasant weather? Praise the Lord anyhow! *"This is the day which the LORD hath made; we will rejoice and be glad in it"* (Psalm 118:24).

6. Do you have true friends who encourage you in times of testing? Then be like Paul; when he saw his friends while being taken to prison in Rome, *"he thanked God, and took courage"* (Acts 28:15). But perhaps you are experiencing "people problems" from those who oppose you, belittle you, or disappoint you. Praise the Lord anyhow!

7. Praise the Lord anyhow! Why? *"We know that all things work together for good to them that love God, to them who are the called according to his purpose"* (Romans 8:28). Don't miss God's plan by praising the Lord only for things you label as blessings. His command is this: *"In every thing give thanks: for this is the will of God in Christ Jesus concerning you"* (1 Thessalonians 5:18).